2021
2022
年度実施

The United Nations
Association's
Test of English

国連英検
過去問題集

公益財団法人
日本国際連合協会 編著

UNA-JAPAN

C級

SANSHUSHA

はじめに
英語コミュニケーション能力の測定と国連英検

国連英検統括監修官　服部孝彦

国連英検は，英語コミュニケーション能力を測るためのテストです。ひとくちにコミュニケーション能力をテストするといっても，「コミュニケーション能力」という概念は複雑です。ここでは，コミュニケーション能力の理論的枠組みをできる限り明らかにし，コミュニケーション能力をより的確に測るためのテストとしての国連英検のあり方について論じます。

1960 年代以降に言語研究に科学的な手法が求められるようになり，「コミュニケーション能力」という概念が生まれました。コミュニケーション能力の概念を最初に示したのはハイムズ（Hymes, 1972）ですが，それ以前に彼は，能力（competence）と運用（performance）の概念を提唱したチョムスキー（Chomsky, 1965）から大きな影響を受けたため，まずチョムスキーの言語理論から考察することにします。

チョムスキーは，従来の学習を習慣形成による刺激と反応の結合が発達したもの，すなわち練習と強化によって形成された習慣とみなす行動主義（behaviorism）の考え方に異論を唱えました。彼は「具体的状況における実際の言語使用」(the actual use of language in concrete situation) を運用（performance）とし，それを「話者—聴者の言語の知識」(the speaker-hearer's knowledge of his language) である能力 (competence) と区別しました。

ハイムズはチョムスキーの能力（competence）の概念を発展させ，コミュニケーション能力 (communicative competence) の概念を示しました。ハイムズは，文法的な意味に限定したチョムスキーの能力（competence）は不十分であるとし，能力を社会的文化的に拡張すると主張しました。ハイムズのコミュニケーション能力は次の 4 つに分類されます。

(1) Whether (and to what degree) something is formally possible;
(2) Whether (and to what degree) something is feasible in virtue of the means of implementation available;
(3) Whether (and to what degree) something is appropriate (adequate, happy, successful) in relation to a context in which it is used and evaluated;
(4) Whether (and to what degree) something is in fact done, actually performed, and what its doing entails.

ハイムズは，文法的に正しいのか，発話することが現実的に可能か，社会的に適切であるか，実際に遂行されているのか，といった４つの基準を示したわけです。前者２つが文法に関するもので，後者２つが発話としての容認性に関するものであるといえます。

ハイムズのコミュニケーション能力は，ウィドウソン（Widdowson, 1983），バックマン（Bachman, 1990），さらにはバックマンとパーマー（Bachman and Palmer, 1996）へと引き継がれました。「コミュニケーション能力」という用語は，communicative competence, communicative language ability, language ability と表記が変わり，定義も見直されました。コミュニケーション能力理論で最も新しいものは，バックマンの論理，およびバックマンとパーマーの理論です。バックマンとパーマー (Bachman and Palmer, 1996）の理論は，バックマン（Bachman, 1990）の理論を踏襲した改訂版で，テスティングのための理論という色彩を強めたものです。この２つの理論は現在，コミュニケーション理論の中で最も信頼のおけるものとして，言語教育で受け入れられています。

バックマンとパーマーは，コミュニケーション能力に language ability という用語を用いています。そして，その language ability の中にハイムズやカネールとスウェインなどが言う communicative competence の構成要素をすべて含んだ言語知識（language knowledge）という概念を設けました。バックマンとパーマーの言語知識は，組織的知識（organizational knowledge）と語用論的知識（pragmatic knowledge）に分けられます。組織的知識はさらに，文法的知識（grammatical knowledge）とテキスト的知識（textual knowledge）に分類されます。語用論的知識は，機能的知識

(functional knowledge) と社会言語学的知識 (sociolinguistic knowledge) に分類されます。バックマンとパーマーは，言語知識以外にトピック知識 (topical knowledge) や個人的特徴 (personal characteristics) なども language ability の中に含まれる要素としており，これらすべてを結びつける能力として方略的能力 (strategic competence) を挙げています。

バックマンとパーマーは次のように述べ，自分たちが提示したコミュニケーションのモデルはテスト開発のためのものである，としています。

> We would note that we conceive of this not as a working model of language processing, but rather as a conceptual basis for organizing our thinking about the test development process.

バックマンとパーマーは，心理的な意味での言語処理モデルではなく，テスト開発のための概念的な枠組みを設定したといえます。

バックマンとパーマーの language ability 理論の基礎になったのが，バックマン (Bachman, 1990) の communicative language ability 理論です。バックマンは，知識 (knowledge) ではなく能力 (competence) という用語を用いて，語用論的能力 (pragmatic competence) と組織的能力 (organizational competence) について，次のように述べています。

> Pragmatic competence includes the types of knowledge which, in addition to organization competence, are employed in the contexturalized performance and interpretation of socially appropriate illocutionary acts in discourse.

ここでバックマンは，語用論的能力／語用論的知識は，組織的能力／組織的知識の基盤の上にできあがるものであることを示しました。また，語用論的能力／語用論的知識は，テキストを構成しない一文単位でも発揮されるということを考えますと，組織的能力／組織的知識の中心は文法的能力／文法的知識であることがわかります。

以上のコミュニケーション能力理論に基づき，国連英検では以下のように出題されています。高等学校で学習する英語の範囲内で出題される C 級は，語用論的知識に先行して学習する必要のある組織的知識について問い，加えて組織的知識の基礎となる文法的知識を中心として出題しています。B級では，組織的知識の中の文法的知識に加え，英文エッセイをテーマに沿って“書く”問題も出題され，組織的知識の中のもう1つの力であるテキスト的知識も問われます。さらに，国連英検の特徴である国連に対する理解についての設問も出されます。特A級とA級では，1次試験の筆記試験で文法的知識とテキスト的知識および国連に関する知識が問われ，1次試験合格者を対象に実施される2次試験の面接テストでは，これらに加えて語用論的知識である機能的知識と社会言語学的知識，言語力の要素を統合させる方略的能力，さらには国際事情についての知識も問われます。

以上のように，国連英検ではコミュニケーション能力の研究成果を踏まえ，コミュニケーション能力の基盤をなす力を下の級で測定し，上の級ではそれらの基盤的な力の測定に加え，語用論的な力とメタ認知方略に関する力も測定しています。特に最上級の特A級では，良識ある国際人として持つべき国際常識や国際適応能力についてもテストされます。国連英検は，まさしく総合的英語コミュニケーション能力を測定する試験であるといえます。

参考文献

Bachman, L. F. (1990). *Fundamental considerations in language testing*. Oxford: Oxford University Press.

Bachman, L. F & Palmer, A. S. (1996). *Language testing in practice*. Oxford: Oxford University Press.

Canale, M. (1983). On some dimensions of language proficiency. In J. Oller (Ed.) *Issues in language testing research*. (pp. 333-387). Massachusetts: Newburry House.

Canale, M. & Swain, M. (1980). Theoretical bases of communicative approaches to second language teaching and testing. *Applied Linguistics, 1* (1), 1-47.

Chomsky, N. (1965). *Aspects of the theory of syntax*. Cambridge, M.A.: The MIT Press.

Hymes, D. (1972). On communicative competence. In J. Pride & J. Holmes (Eds.) *Sociolinguistics: Selected readings*. (pp. 269-293). Harmondsworth: Penguin.

Widdowson, H. G. (1983). *Learning purpose and language use*. Oxford: Oxford University Press.

国連英検過去問題集　C級（2021-2022実施）

目次

※本書は，実際の検定試験で使用された試験問題に基づいて編集されておりますが，一部修正されている場合があります。

国連英検とは

■「国連英検」（国際連合公用語英語検定試験）は，1981 年に始まり，長い歴史を持つ英語検定試験です。試験は年に 2 回，全国主要都市で実施されます。特 A 級から E 級まで全部で 6 つの級があり（注：現在 D 級・E 級は休止中），中学生から社会人，シニアエイジまでの幅広い層を対象とし，受験資格は特になく，どなたでも受験できます。

試験を主催するのは，外務省の外郭団体としてスタートした公益財団法人日本国際連合協会です。日本国際連合協会は，国連の A 級諮問民間団体である「国連協会世界連盟」（WFUNA）の有力メンバーで，国内外での国連普及活動を積極的に行っています。

国連英検も国連普及活動の一環として実施されており，国連の理念である「国際協力」「国際理解」をコンセプトに，「真に役立つグローバルコミュニケーション能力」の育成を目標としています。試験内容は国連の活動に沿って，世界平和，地球環境，世界政治，世界経済から，人権，食品，医療などの世界情勢，国際時事問題まで幅広く出題されるため，今まさに地球上で問われている問題を認識し，自分の考えや解決策を論理的に伝達する表現力が求められます。単なる語学力の判定にとどまらず，総合的な国際コミュニケーションスキルが問われます。

■ 国連英検は，資格として多角的にアピールできる検定試験です。多くの大学で推薦入試・編入試験の評価資格として認められ，B 級以上の合格を単位認定している大学もあります。

特 A 級は，成績優秀者に外務大臣賞が授与されるほか，合格者には外務省国際機関人事センターが実施している「JPO 派遣候補者選考試験」において加点が行われます。

この JPO は，国際公務員（国連職員・ユネスコ職員など）になるための登竜門と言えるもので，2 年間の海外派遣を経て国際公務員試験に挑戦できる制度です。

A 級は成績優秀者に国連協会会長賞が授与されます。

C 級以上の合格者は，文部科学省より，高等学校卒業程度認定規則において，英語資格としてレベル認定されています。

また，国際協力機構（JICA）では，C 級以上の合格者を，応募の際に必要となる語学力の評価基準をクリアしたものと認定しています。

なお，警視庁では警察官採用試験（1 次試験）に「資格経歴等の評定」を導入していますが，国連英検 C 級以上の合格者については，1 次試験の成績の一部として評価しています。

■ 国連英検は，コミュニケーションを重視した試験です。B 級～ E 級で出題されるリスニング問題のウェイトは 40%と高く，また B 級以上は国際時事問題をテーマとした英作文（ウェイト 20%）が設けられています。A 級以上は 2 次試験で面接試験を実施し，ネイティブスピーカーと国際時事問題について討論を行います。さらに特 A 級については，ネイティブスピーカーに加え，元外務省大使など外交実務経験者や国際関係を研究する大学教授を面接官として，より深い議論を行います。

●国連英検 D 級・E 級の開催休止について

国連英検では昨今の英語教育における新学習指導要領の大幅な改定に鑑み，主に中学生～高校生を受験対象としている D 級・E 級の試験実施を 2023 年度より休止しています。再開時期・受験形式等は，決定次第国連英検のホームページにて広報致します。

●国連英検受験のための指定テキストについて

国連英検は国連に関する基礎知識を学習するための教材として『新 わかりやすい国連の活動と世界』（三修社）を指定テキストとし，特 A 級～ C 級の出題にも使用しています。級により出題範囲が異なりますので，事前にホームページで確認することをお勧めします。

● C級のレベルと審査基準および問題の傾向と対策 ●

レベルと審査基準

問題の形式と内容が異なるため，他の英語検定試験との比較は困難ですが，国連英検Ｃ級は実用英語検定２級とほぼ同じ，あるいはそれより高いレベルといってよいでしょう。内容的には高校修了程度の英語力を基準にして，標準的な大学入試問題に実用英語をプラスしたものです。文法は文部科学省の学習指導要領を基準に，語彙《ごい》は基本的な3000語程度を用い，高度で難解な語句には日本語の脚注がつきます。日常生活における会話文や頻繁に用いられる表現，状況に応じて英語で応対する能力，ノンフィクションのなかでも時事的な内容，国連に関する内容，随筆，フィクションでは短編小説などが理解できる読解力が要求されます。

問題の傾向と対策

試験はまずリスニングテスト（40点）で始まり，マークシートによる客観テスト（60点）が続きます。（英作文，２次試験はありません）。

リスニングテストのトピックには，短い対話や200語程度の物語やエッセイが用いられ，大問４題が出題されます。大意が楽に読み取れる程度の英文を多く読み，ラジオやテレビの英語講座や国連英検の過去問題集などで英語を聴き取る練習を数多く行うことが大切です。

客観テストでは大問６問で，短文による表現力，文型，文法，語彙をテストする問題と，250～300語前後の会話，物語，エッセイ，時事論説などの内容を理解する読解力をテストする問題で構成されます。学生・一般社会人向けの英字新聞やペーパーバックなどを読む必要があります。また，Ｃ級以上は国連の活動を報じる文章も出題されるため，Ｃ級受験者も指定テキスト『新 わかりやすい国連の活動と世界』*New Today's Guide to the United Nations*（三修社）を読んでおくことが大切です。各級の指定テキストからの出題範囲は国連英検のホームページに掲載されています。

2021年

第1回試験

問題

C級試験問題用紙

C級

外務省後援

２０２１年度第１回国際連合公用語

英語検定試験（100分）

受験上の注意

1. 問題用紙は試験開始の合図があるまで開いてはいけません。その間に、この**受験上の注意を熟読しておいてください。**
2. **受験番号と氏名を解答用紙（マークシート）**に記入してください。
3. 解答用紙の配布は１人１部のみです。複数の配布は致しません。
4. 試験開始前は、答案への解答記入は禁止です。
5. マークシートの記入は、必ずＨＢ以上の濃い鉛筆を使って該当箇所を黒く塗りつぶしてください。書き間違いの場合は「アト」が残らないように消してください。マークシートは絶対に折ったり曲げたりしないでください。
6. 受験級、受験地区、会場番号、受験番号のマークシートへの記入は監督者の指示に従い、間違いなく記入してください。**（裏表紙の「マークシート記入例」参照）**
7. 試験問題についての質問は、印刷が不鮮明な場合を除き、一切受けつけません。
8. 中途退室の際は、マークシートを監督者に渡し、他の受験者の迷惑にならないように静かに退室してください。中途退室後の再入室はできません。
9. 試験中は他の受験者の妨げとなる行動は慎んでください。また携帯電話等の電源はお切りください。
10. マークシートは監督者に提出し、問題用紙はご自由にお持ち帰りください。

＊試験問題の複製や転載、インターネットへのアップロード等、いかなる媒体への転用を禁止します。

リスニングテストについて

1. リスニングテストは試験開始後、合図があってから実施されます。(40問あります)
2. リスニングテストが始まる前にリスニング問題の指示と内容を読んで、どういう形式のテストなのか、概要をつかんでおいてください。
3. テスト中の発言は、放送機器の具合が悪く放送された英語の聴き取りができない場合を除いて、しないようにしてください。

試験結果について

1. 試験の結果は2021年６月30日㈬頃に通知します。
2. その間に住所変更をされた方は、郵便局へ住所変更の届け出を忘れずに行ってください。
3. 発表前の試験結果のお問合せには応じられません。

UNA-JAPAN
公益財団法人 日本国際連合協会
http://www.unaj.or.jp/

I. これから短い英文を10言います。英文は２回言います。よく聞いて、会話が成り立つように最も適切なものをA、B、C、Dの中から１つ選びなさい。途中でメモを取ってもかまいません。

1. A. It's expensive. B. He'll call you soon.
C. Take it easy. D. Here you are.

2. A. I'd love to. B. I study every day.
C. I like music. D. Don't worry about it.

3. A. It's long.
B. You can keep it until you're done with it.
C. It's sold at the bookstore.
D. I'll finish my assignment.

4. A. I like to keep the room tidy. B. I like to live in a big house.
C. I like neither of them. D. I don't want to design them.

5. A. I'm using a pay phone. B. I'm smarter than you.
C. You should get more exercise. D. Be careful in what you select.

6. A. Have you seen apple flowers? B. They have no chemicals.
C. I should buy some more of them. D. Would you like to eat them?

7. A. Two days after tomorrow. B. Is it difficult?
C. You can finish mine. D. I will stay up late tonight.

8. A. I like to travel. B. I'm looking forward to it.
C. I like spicy food. D. I love music.

9. A. I had some popcorn.
B. I saw many people in the movie theater.
C. It was exciting.
D. I saw the movie yesterday.

10. A. I'm bored.
B. You should not brag about it.
C. I have many options.
D. Consider if it's important for your future.

Ⅱ. これから短い会話を10言います。会話は2回繰り返します。そのあと、会話の内容について10の質問をします。質問も2回繰り返します。よく聞いて、それぞれの質問の答えとして最も適切なものをA、B、C、Dの中から1つ選びなさい。途中でメモを取ってもかまいません。

11. A. It's strongly made.
B. It starts to look bad quickly.
C. It's too expensive.
D. It's poorly made.

12. A. He wants to drink apple juice.
B. He wants to drink tea.
C. He wants to drink apple juice and tea.
D. He is deciding whether to have apple juice or tea.

13. A. Besides, he is indecisive.
B. Besides, he is modest.
C. Besides, he is boastful.
D. Besides, he is forgetful.

14. A. He doesn't want to work hard.
B. He wants to forget about his work.
C. He doesn't want to delay his work.
D. He doesn't like to plan his work.

15. A. It's broken.
B. It's stolen.
C. It's new.
D. It's the best.

16. A. He'll photograph her suitcase.
B. He'll watch her suitcase.
C. He'll give her suitcase away.
D. He'll steal her suitcase.

17. A. She'll look for his coffee cup.
B. She'll have some coffee with him.
C. She'll make some coffee for him.
D. She'll give him a new coffee cup.

18. A. She's an excellent pianist.
B. She cannot play the piano.
C. She's not a bad pianist.
D. Someday she might become a good pianist.

19. A. He shouldn't bother with his doctor.
B. He should help his doctor.
C. He should see his doctor.
D. He should avoid his doctor.

20. A. He's happy his friend will visit him.
B. He's glad her family stayed with him.
C. He's grateful to her family for letting him stay with them.
D. He's surprised her family visited him.

Ⅲ. これから英文を2回繰り返します。そのあと、内容について10の質問をします。質問も2回繰り返します。よく聞いて、それぞれの質問の答えとして最も適切なものをA、B、C、Dの中から1つ選びなさい。途中でメモを取ってもかまいません。

21. A. Six years ago. B. Ten years ago.
C. Thirty years ago. D. Forty years ago.

22. A. Japanese literature. B. English literature.
C. English conversation. D. American history.

23. A. At a university. B. At a high school.
C. In club activities. D. In a writing class.

24. A. To study harder.
B. To consider ideas for their future.
C. To graduate quickly.
D. To go on to a graduate school.

25. A. To become a writer.
B. To get to know her classmates.
C. To major in Japanese literature.
D. To become a professor.

26. A. She didn't understand.
B. She was extremely disappointed.
C. She didn't care.
D. She would change her mind to become a writer.

27. A. Keep doing what she loves to do.
B. Give up doing what she likes to do.
C. Save money for her future.
D. Keep writing in her diaries.

28. A. She passed the test for a company.
B. She entered a Japanese university.
C. She was accepted by a graduate school in America.
D. She got a scholarship from a Japanese university.

29. A. She became very busy with her academic work in America.
B. She simply forgot about him.
C. She thought he was boring.
D. She thought he did not like her.

30. A. He became a great writer.
B. He became a professor.
C. He gave up his hope.
D. He went to America.

Ⅳ. これから会話を２回繰り返します。そのあと、内容について10の質問をします。質問も２回繰り返します。よく聞いて、それぞれの質問の答えとして最も適切なものをA、B、C、Dの中から１つ選びなさい。途中でメモを取ってもかまいません。

31. A. She is indecisive.
B. She is unwilling to answer.
C. She has two opposite opinions.
D. She did not understand Jim's question.

32. A. Students ask many questions.
B. Teachers can check students' attendance easily.
C. Students don't use the chat function.
D. Teachers can demand a lot of work from students.

33. A. He feels online classes are hard to control.
B. He feels students are more motivated.
C. He wants to experience online classes.
D. He wants to use the chat function.

34. A. Not sharing their opinions.
B. Taking photos.
C. Presenting their assignments using slides.
D. Giving assignments to other students.

35. A. Quality of their work. B. Quantity of their work.
C. How much they can share. D. Meeting a deadline.

36. A. About twenty. B. About thirty.
C. About forty. D. About fifty or more.

37. A. Remember students' names.
B. Evaluate students' accomplishments individually.
C. Giving students assignments.
D. Collecting students' assignments.

38. A. Give students a comprehension test.
B. Give makeup classes.
C. Give presentations.
D. Give students a lecture.

39. A. She doesn't think it is useful.
B. She thinks Jim should try it.
C. She will try it.
D. She will think up something else.

40. A. English. B. Photography.
C. Nursing. D. It is not stated.

V. 次の英文の下線部の意味を最もよく表す語または語句をA、B、C、Dの中から1つ選びなさい。

41. She has a heart of gold.
A. is shining B. is kind
C. has a lot of gold D. has a cold heart

42. Business was hard hit during the pandemic.
A. made a record B. made a hit
C. stayed the same D. suffered

43. His efforts went for nothing.
A. were useful for something B. were interesting
C. were in vain D. became famous

44. You must hand in your assignment tomorrow.

A. write by hand　　B. copy

C. discuss　　D. submit

45. Talking to him was like talking to a wall.

A. necessary　　B. beneficial　　C. useless　　D. worthwhile

46. She walked away from the difficult task.

A. abandoned　　B. planned

C. requested　　D. experimented

47. Let's take five.

A. go　　B. take a break

C. get to work　　D. work until five o'clock

48. He gave her a whole bunch of flowers.

A. several fresh　　B. a few

C. some bright　　D. a lot of

49. She is always keeping up appearances.

A. pretending　　B. visiting her family

C. telling the truth　　D. singing well

50. Could you dispose of the garbage?

A. lighten up　　B. freeze

C. line up　　D. get rid of

VI. 次の英文を読み、設問の答えとして最も適切なものをA、B、C、Dの中から1つ選びなさい。

The General Assembly has no power to *compel any government to take any action. Its influence is **(56)** exercised through the weight of its recommendations as an expression of world opinion.

The General Assembly may discuss any issue coming within the **(57)** scope of the Charter of the United Nations or concerning any **(58)** body established under the Charter. It may make recommendations to Member States or to the Security Council or to both, with one exception—it may not make recommendations on any **(59)** dispute or situation which the Council currently has under consideration, unless the Security Council so requests.

The General Assembly may consider the general principles of cooperation for maintaining peace and security, including those governing *disarmament and the regulation of arms. It may discuss any issue concerning peace and security that is brought before it by a Member State, the Security Council or a nonmember state, if that State accepts in advance the obligations of peaceful **(60)** settlement contained in the Charter. Unless the matter is already being dealt with by the Security Council, the Assembly may make recommendations to the State or States concerned or to the Security Council or to both.

The finances of the United Nations are controlled by the General Assembly, which approves the regular budget and *apportions the expenses among the Members. It also examines the administrative budgets of the specialized agencies.

The General Assembly meets once a year in regular session, *commencing on the third Tuesday in September and continuing until mid-December. The regular session may sometimes be resumed again the following year. Special sessions may be called at the request of the Security Council, of a majority of Member States, as well as at the request of one Member State with the *concurrence of a majority. An emergency special session may be called within 24 hours of a request by the Security Council on the vote of any nine of its members, or by a majority of Member States.

注）*compel　強制する　　*disarmament　軍備縮小　　*apportion　割り当てる
*commence　始める　　*concurrence　同意

51. What does the General Assembly NOT force any government to do?

A. To cooperate with each other.　　B. To maintain peace.
C. To take action.　　D. To ignore each other.

52. What issues does the General Assembly take up to discuss?

A. Issues that are not in the scope of the Charter of the United Nations.
B. Issues within the scope of the Charter of the United Nations.
C. Issues that have nothing to do with the United Nations system.
D. Issues concerning a particular government.

53. What is one of the systems that plays a role for prompting the General Assembly to discuss issues concerning peace and security?

A. A Member State.　　B. Any kind of government.
C. World's most important countries.　　D. World Trade Organization.

54. What organization inspects the administrative budgets of the specialized agencies?

A. The General Assembly.　　B. The Security Council.
C. The Economic and Social Council.　　D. The Trusteeship Council.

55. What is NOT true according to the text?

A. The General Assembly meets once a year in regular session.
B. The regular session sometimes resumes again the following year.
C. Special sessions may not be called at any time.
D. An emergency special session may be called within 24 hours.

56. What does the underlined part (56) exercised mean?

A. talked about B. carried out
C. taken up D. ruled out

57. What does the underlined part (57) scope mean?

A. glass B. observation
C. range D. investigation

58. What does the underlined part (58) body mean?

A. agency B. figure
C. burden D. negotiation

59. What does the underlined part (59) dispute mean?

A. profit B. response
C. disagreement D. classification

60. What does the underlined part (60) settlement mean?

A. ignorance B. formula
C. exhibition D. agreement

Ⅶ. 次の各組の文の空所には同じ語が入ります。最も適切なものをA、B、C、Dの中から1つ選びなさい。

61. She ________ the school record in running. He went ________ by selling used cars.

A. lost B. broke C. home D. down

62. I need a ________ of bread. He wants to ________ today.

A. jog B. head C. work D. loaf

63. The jazz musicians took some ________. There are ________ in the walls.

A. breaks B. rests C. drinks D. snacks

64. **They tried to ________ their way in. The ________ of Earth's gravity is moderate.**

A. push B. force C. fly D. fix

65. **I need to ________ some money. The tennis match was a ________.**

A. draw B. save C. tie D. dream

66. **Please ________ the form. I needed one ________ year to finish the work.**

A. fill B. extra C. complete D. add

67. **Will you ________ this message to her? I must put my watch ________ .**

A. send B. forward C. attach D. spend

68. **She made a speech to ________ her gratitude. I took the ________ train.**

A. express B. introduce C. describe D. fast

69. **She wanted to ________ the lost dog. Food, clothing and ________ are our necessities.**

A. protect B. shelter C. furniture D. housing

70. **The writer likes to ________ his essays on his website. She took up a ________ at the company.**

A. write B. job C. keep D. post

Ⅷ. 次のA、B、C、Dからなる各組の英文には下線部に誤りを含むものが1つあります。その文を選びなさい。

71. A. Is this coffee for here, or to go?
B. Let go the rope.
C. Could you go over the report?
D. I had to go without the Internet for a week.

72. A. I set the alarm clock for seven.
B. He had to work hard against the clock.
C. She always beats the clock.
D. The store is open around clock.

73. A. The restaurant is back on business.
B. He got down to business after his vacation.
C. She has no business telling you what to do.
D. The hotel went out of business last year.

74. A. I have to open an account with the bank.
B. Don't worry on my account.
C. She is competent in her own account.
D. He does the accounts at the company.

75. A. She has to put her children to bed at nine.
B. He took in his bed in his late life.
C. The situation was like a bed of nails.
D. It's time to go to bed.

76. A. Please go on the board the ferryboat.
B. He put an onion on the cutting board.
C. She is on the board of managers.
D. I need to board up the windows for the storm.

77. A. Let's get to the bottom of the problem.
B. He thanked people from the bottom of his heart.
C. Please write your address at the bottom of the form.
D. Bottom up!

78. A. He is good at oil painting.
B. He burnt the midnight oils.
C. They are like oil and water.
D. Don't pour oil on troubled water.

79. A. Please pass on the information to your friends.
B. He passed out during the meeting.
C. She passed away the invitation to the banquet.
D. The famous singer passed away due to natural causes.

80. A. She made the most of her time.
B. He likes reading mysteries most of all.
C. It will take two hours at most.
D. Most of students were in the classroom.

IX. 次の英文を読み、設問の答として最も適切なものをA、B、C、Dの中から1つ選びなさい。

"*Touchdown confirmed: There's a new robot on the surface of *Mars."

The American space agency has successfully landed its *Perseverance Mars rover on the surface of Mars in a deep *crater near the planet's *equator called Jezero.

"The good news is the *spacecraft is in great shape," said Matt Wallace, the mission's deputy project manager.

Engineers at NASA's mission control in California *erupted with joy when the confirmation of touchdown came through.

The six-wheeled vehicle will now spend at least the next two years drilling into the local rocks, looking for evidence of past life.

Jezero is thought to have held a giant lake billions of years ago. And where there's been water, there's the possibility there might also have been life.

The signal *alerting controllers that Perseverance was down and safe arrived at 20:55 GMT. In the past they might have hugged or *high-fived but strict coronavirus *protocols meant they had all been separated by *Perspex screens. A *respectful fist bump was about all they could manage.

*Nonetheless, the excitement was evident. And the applause continued when the first two images came in. There was dust covering the *still-attached *translucent lens covers, but it was possible to see a flat surface both in front and behind the rover.

*Post-landing analysis indicated the vehicle had come down about 2 km to the south east of the *delta feature in Jezero that Perseverance plans to investigate.

"We are in a nice flat spot. The vehicle is only *tilted by about 1.2 degrees," said Allen Chen, who led the landing team. "So we did successfully find that parking lot and have a safe rover on the ground. And I couldn't be more proud of my team for doing that."

*Steve Jurczyk, the acting administrator at NASA, also *saluted the achievement: "What a credit to the team. Just what an amazing team to work through all the *adversity and all the challenges that go with landing a rover on Mars, plus the challenges of COVID-19. Just an amazing accomplishment."

注）*touchdown　着陸　　*Mars　火星
*Perseverance Mars rover　火星探査車パーシビアランス
*crater　火口状のくぼみ、クレーター　　*equator　赤道
*spacecraft　宇宙船　　*erupt　（感情が）爆発する
*alert　注意を喚起する　　*high-five　ハイタッチする
*protocol　感染対策、感染防止対処方針
*Perspex　パースペックス（頑丈な透明アクリル樹脂）
*respectful　礼儀正しい　　*nonetheless　それにもかかわらず

*still-attached　まだ付属している　*translucent　半透明の
*post-landing　着陸後の　*delta　三角州　*tilt　傾く
*Steve Jurczyk, the acting administrator　スティーブ・ジャージック長官代行
*salute　敬意を表する、たたえる　*adversity　逆境

81. **"Touchdown confirmed: There's a new robot on the surface of Mars." What does this mean?**

A. The Perseverance rover crash landed on Mars.
B. The Perseverance rover flew by Mars into outer space.
C. The Perseverance rover touched down on Mars and flew back to Earth.
D. The Perseverance rover landed successfully in a Mars crater.

82. **What is "Jezero"?**

A. The American space agency headquarters in Southern California.
B. The name of the Perseverance rover.
C. The name of the crater where Perseverance rover landed.
D. An animal that lives in the crater.

83. **How many years will the six-wheeled Mars rover spend drilling in rocks?**

A. One year.　B. Two years.　C. Ten years.　D. Forever.

84. **What will the rover vehicle be looking for in the Jezero crater?**

A. Signs of past ancient life from billions of years ago.
B. Signs of present-day suburban life on Mars.
C. Signs of gold, diamonds and oil wells.
D. All of the above.

85. **What might have the crater contained billions of years ago?**

A. A lake.　B. A desert.　C. Snow.　D. People.

86. **How did the American space agency personnel react to the rover landing?**

A. They were very disappointed.
B. They hugged and "high-fived" each other.
C. Because of COVID-19 they had to be subdued and be separated behind Perspex screens.
D. They got drunk and had a "Mars party."

87. What were the American space agency personnel first able to see clearly of the Mars surface?

A. Nothing.

B. The view from the front and back of the rover.

C. A lake.

D. People from Mars.

88. Alen Chen said: "I couldn't be more proud of my team doing that." What did he mean?

A. He had a good time going to Mars.

B. Though it was very difficult; the team landed the Mars rover perfectly with only a minor tilt.

C. The team was very brave when the whole mission failed.

D. Fortunately someone on the team was able to communicate with the people on Mars.

89. What challenges in regard to COVID-19 does Steve Jurczyk refer to?

A. Being extra careful with each other while paying close attention to the Mars lander.

B. Caring about the Mars lander only.

C. Caring about teams only.

D. Making sure COVID-19 did not spread to the people on Mars.

90. What is the best title for this story?

A. The Failure of the Mars Lander

B. Let's Go to Mars Together!

C. Mars Lander Succeeds in Spite of Major Difficulties

D. The Mars Lander Goes to the Moon

X. 次の会話を読み、設問の答として最も適切なものをA、B、C、Dの中から１つ選びなさい。

Jane : Hi, Bob. Do you like chocolate?

Bob : Hi, Jane. Yes, I do love it. Generally, I don't like sweets, but chocolate is an exception.

Jane : Would you like to try this chocolate?

Bob : Oh, sure. Thanks.

Jane : How is it?

Bob : I've never tasted anything like this. This is the best I've ever had. I wonder why it tastes so great.

Jane : Actually, this chocolate is organic and a Fairtrade product.

Bob : I understand "organic" but what does "Fairtrade" mean?

Jane : Have you seen this mark?

Bob : No, I haven't. This is the first time I've noticed the mark on the label.

Jane : Well, this is one of the marks of Fairtrade. It means this product was produced according to the Fairtrade's policies.

Bob : What are its policies?

Jane : In short, the Fairtrade products are focused on "better prices, decent working conditions and a fairer deal for farmers and workers in developing countries" according to its homepage.

Bob : It sounds **(99)** beneficial for both farmers and consumers.

Jane : That's exactly right. If we support Fairtrade products, we can save farmers and workers, including children from unfair working conditions.

Bob : How is the standard set to qualify being a product as a Fairtrade product?

Jane : There are three criteria: economic, environmental and social.

Bob : Could you explain them in concrete?

Jane : The economic criteria include the Fairtrade Minimum Price which aims to provide producers with a safety net against falling prices and allow long-term planning, along with a fixed Fairtrade Premium that provides farmers and workers with additional money to invest in improving the quality of their businesses and communities.

Bob : What about the environmental criteria?

Jane : The environmental criteria emphasize *ecologically and agriculturally **(100)** sound practices. Fairtrade prohibits the use of several *hazardous materials and all *genetically modified organisms (GMOs).

Bob : Could you tell me about the social criteria?

Jane : The social criteria for small-scale producers include requirements on democratic self-organization, typically in *cooperatives, *participatory *decision-making, transparency, and non-discrimination, including gender *equity. In plantation-type settings where hired labor is the *norm, our standards require companies to operate with non-discriminatory employment practices, pay rates equal to or higher than the legal or regional minimum wages, freedom of association and *collective bargaining rights for the *workforce, *safeguards for worker safety and health, and facilities to allow workers to manage the Fairtrade *Premium. Forced labor and child labor are prohibited under the Fairtrade Standards.

Bob : Thank you so much for introducing me to the Fairtrade production. I will look for the marks next time I shop.

注) *ecologically　生態学的に　　*hazardous　有害な
*genetically modified organisms (GMOs)　遺伝子組換え生物

*cooperative　協同組合　　*participatory　参加型
*decision-making　意思決定　　*equity　公平、公正
*norm　標準、ふつうの　　*collective bargaining　団体交渉
*workforce従業員　　*safeguard　保護手段
*premium　賞、ほうび、奨励金

91. What is one of the characteristics of the chocolate that Jane offers to Bob?

A. Its ingredient is artificial.　B. It was produced by forced labor.
C. It was made using GMOs.　D. It is a Fairtrade product.

92. How can a consumer tell that a chocolate is a Fairtrade product?

A. By its color.　B. By word of mouth.
C. By eating it.　D. By a mark on its label.

93. What is one of the Fairtrade's policies?

A. Comfortable working conditions.　B. Low prices.
C. Fairer deals for employers.　D. Unfair working conditions.

94. What are the criteria for Fairtrade products?

A. Insurance, popularity and images.
B. Economic, environmental and social criteria.
C. Creativity, academic achievements and test scores.
D. Political belief, profits and quantity.

95. What is NOT true about the economic criteria?

A. Fairtrade Minimum Price aims to provide producers with a safety net against rising prices.
B. Fairtrade Minimum Price allows long-term planning.
C. A fixed Fairtrade Premium provides farmers and workers with additional money.
D. A fixed Fairtrade Premium's additional money is to invest in improving the quality of their businesses and communities.

96. What is NOT true about the environmental criteria?

A. They focus on sound ecological practices.
B. They emphasize sound agricultural practices.
C. They encourage the use of genetically modified organisms.
D. They forbid the use of several hazardous materials.

97. What is NOT true about the social criteria?

A. They include requirements on democratic self-organization and non-discrimination.

B. They require companies to operate with non-discriminatory employment practices.

C. They require companies to provide safeguards for worker safety and health.

D. They don't allow companies to pay attention to pay rates equal to or higher than the legal or regional minimum wages.

98. How is Bob feeling after learning about Fairtrade policies?

A. He has lost interest in chocolate.

B. He is willing to support Fairtrade products.

C. He is feeling that it has nothing to do with him.

D. He is hoping that Jane will buy more chocolate for him.

99. What does the underlined word (99) beneficial mean?

A. useless　　B. competitive

C. rational　　D. good

100. What does the underlined word (100) sound mean?

A. noisy　　B. quiet

C. appropriate　　D. incapable

マークシート記入例

東京の本会場でC級を受験する、国連 太郎さん、受験番号が「東京01-40001」、生年月日が「1980年10月24日」の場合の記入例です。

【受験番号/氏名】
それぞれ受験票の記載通りに記入してください。

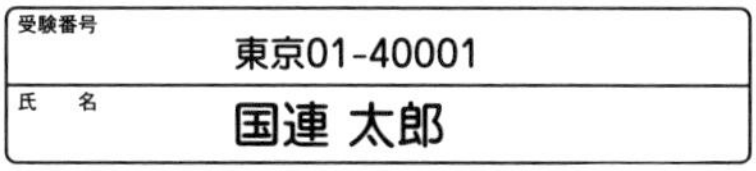

【受験地区】
下段の都道府県部分を塗りつぶしてください。

【会場番号】
都道府県部分に続く２桁の数字を塗りつぶしてください。

【受験番号】
ハイフン（－）以降の５桁の数字を塗りつぶしてください。

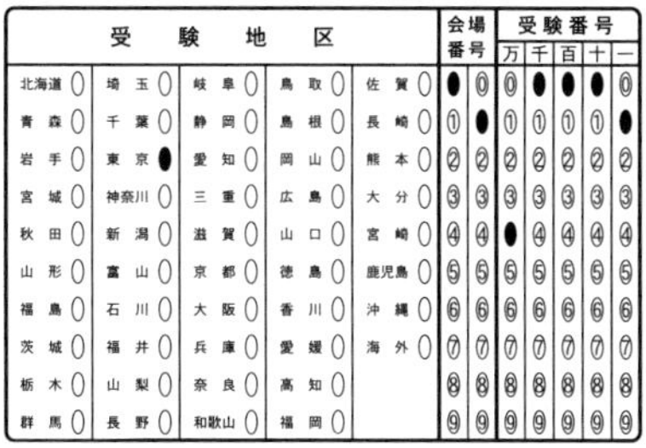

【受験級】
「C」と記入し、下段のC級部分を塗りつぶしてください。

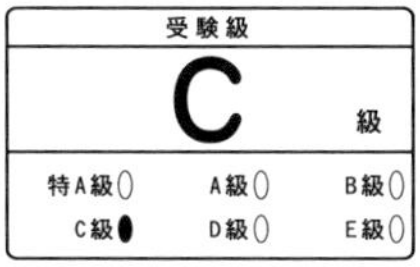

【生年月日】
４桁の西暦・月・日を塗りつぶしてください。
10未満の月・日の十の位は、「０」を塗りつぶしてください。

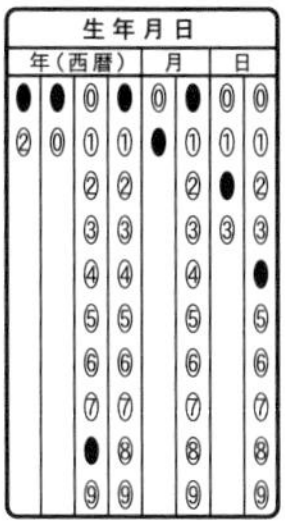

※HB以上の鉛筆を用いてマークをしてください。

※他の地区から会場を変更して受験する場合でも、受験票に記載されている受験地区・会場番号をマークしてください。

2021年
第1回試験
解答・解説

2021年　国連英検C級第1回試験
解答・解説

I　短い英文を2度聴いたあと，
その英文に対して適切な応答を選ぶリスニングテスト。10問出題。

1.　解答：C

解説　話者は予定が詰まっていることを伝えているので，選択肢の中で最もふさわしい応答は，Cが正解。

ナレーション　I have a full schedule this week.
「私は今週予定がきっしり詰まっています」
A. それは高価です。　B. 彼はあなたにすぐ電話するでしょう。
C. 無理しないでね。　D. はいどうぞ。

2.　解答：A

解説　話者は相手に散歩をしたいかどうか尋ねているので，選択肢の中で最もふさわしい応答は，Aが正解。

ナレーション　Would you like to take a walk to the beach?
「海辺まで散歩しませんか」
A. 喜んで。　B. 私は毎日勉強します。
C. 私は音楽が好きです。　D. そのことは心配しないでください。

3.　解答：B

解説　話者は相手から借りている本を返すタイミングを尋ねているので，選択肢の中で最もふさわしい応答は，Bが正解。

ナレーション　When shall I return this book to you?
「この本をいつあなたにお返ししましょうか」
A. それは長いです。　B. それを読み終えるまで持っていていいですよ。
C. それは書店で売っています。　D. 私は宿題を終えるつもりです。

4. 解答：C

解説 話者は相手に２つのカバンのうち好きな方を尋ねているので，選択肢の中で最もふさわしい応答は，C が正解。

ナレーション Which bag do you like better?
「どちらのカバンが好きですか」
A. 私は部屋を片付けておくのが好きです。
B. 私は大きな家に住むのが好きです。
C. 私はどちらも好きではありません。
D. 私はそれらのデザインはしたくありません。

5. 解答：D

解説 話者は相手に最新のスマートフォンを購入すると伝えているので，選択肢の中で最もふさわしい応答は，D が正解。

ナレーション I'm thinking of buying the latest smartphone.
「私は最新のスマートフォンを買うつもりです」
A. 私は公衆電話を使っています。
B. 私はあなたより賢い。
C. あなたはもっと運動をすべきです。
D. あなたは注意して選んでください。

6. 解答：B

解説 話者は相手にそれらのリンゴが好きな理由を尋ねているので，選択肢の中で最もふさわしい応答は，B が正解。

ナレーション Why do you like these apples?
「あなたはなぜこれらのリンゴが好きなのですか」
A. あなたはリンゴの花を見たことがありますか。
B. それらには化学物質が一切使用されていません。
C. わたしはそれらをもっと買うべきです。
D. あなたはそれらを食べたいですか。

7. 解答：A

解説 話者は相手に宿題の提出期限を尋ねているので，選択肢の中で最もふさわしい応答は，A が正解。

ナレーション　When is this homework due?

「この宿題の締め切りはいつですか」

A. 3 日後

B. それは難しいですか。

C. あなたは私のを仕上げてください。

D. 私は今夜は遅くまで起きています。

8. 解答：B

解説 話者は相手に次の休暇で再び会えると伝えているので，選択肢の中で最もふさわしい応答は，B が正解。

ナレーション　I'll see you again next vacation.

「私は次の休暇であなたにまたお会いしましょう」

A. 私は旅行が好きです。　B. 私はそれを楽しみにしています。

C. 私はスパイスのきいた食べ物が好きです。　D. 私は音楽が好きです。

9. 解答：C

解説 話者は相手に映画の感想を尋ねているので，選択肢の中で最もふさわしい応答は，C が正解。

ナレーション　How did you like the movie?

「映画はどうでしたか」

A. 私はポップコーンを食べました。

B. 私は映画館でたくさんの人を見ました。

C. それは面白かった。

D. 私は昨日その映画を見ました。

10. 解答：D

解説 話者は相手に大学進学を迷っていると伝えているので，選択肢の中で最もふさわしい応答は，D が正解。

ナレーション　I'm not sure whether to go on to a university.

「私は大学に進学すべきかどうか迷っています」

A. 私は退屈しています。

B. あなたはそれを自慢してはいけません。

C. 私にはたくさんの選択肢があります。

D. 自分の将来にとってそれが重要かどうかを考えてください。

II 短い会話を２度聴いたあと，その内容に関する質問を聴いて答えるリスニングテスト。10問出題。

11. 解答：A

解説 Wear out は「すり減る」の意味で，女性はカバンが頑丈にできていると言っている。A が正解。

A. それは頑丈に作られている。　B. それはすぐに見かけが悪くなる。

C. それは高価すぎる。　D. それは雑に作られている。

ナレーション

Man:　I like this leather bag.

Woman: It doesn't wear out so easily.

Question　What does the woman mean?

（男）：僕はこの革のバッグが好きなんだ。

（女）：そう簡単にすり減らないわね。

質問　女性は何と言っていますか。

12. 解答：D

解説 be torn between は「どちらを選択するのか迷っている」の意味で，男性はリンゴジュースとお茶の選択に迷っていると言っている。D が正解。

A. 彼はリンゴジュースが飲みたい。

B. 彼はお茶が飲みたい。

C. 彼はリンゴジュースとお茶が飲みたい。

D. 彼はリンゴジュースとお茶のどちらにするのか決めているところだ。

ナレーション

Woman: What would you like to drink?

Man:　I'm torn between apple juice and tea.

Question　What does the man mean?

（女）：お飲み物は何になさいますか。

（男）：リンゴジュースとお茶のどちらにするのか迷っています。

質問　男性は何と言っていますか。

13. 解答：B

解説 show off は「ひけらかす」の意味で，ひけらかすことが嫌いな人と言っている。B が正解。

A. その上彼は優柔不断だ。　B. その上彼は控え目だ。

C. その上彼は自慢したがる。　D. その上彼は忘れっぽい。

ナレーション

Man:　He is a very accomplished scientist.

Woman: Besides, he doesn't like to show off.

Question　What does the woman mean?

(男)：彼はとても優れた科学者だ。

(女)：その上彼はひけらかすことが好きではないわ。

質問　女性は何と言っていますか。

14. 解答：C

解説 put off は「延期する」の意味で，仕事を遅らせるのが嫌だと言っている。C が正解。

A. 彼は一生懸命に働きたくない。　B. 彼は仕事のことを忘れたい。

C. 彼は仕事を遅らせたくない。　D. 彼は仕事の計画を立てたくない。

ナレーション

Woman: You're working hard today.

Man:　I don't like to put off my work.

Question　What does the man mean?

(女)：今日は一生懸命働いているのね。

(男)：僕は仕事を延期するのが嫌いなんだ。

質問　男性は何と言っていますか。

15. 解答：A

解説 out of order は「故障して」の意味で，女性は機械が故障していると言っている。A が正解。

A. それは壊れている。　B. それは盗まれた。

C. それは新しい。　D. それは最良だ。

ナレーション

Man:　I wonder why the machine doesn't work.

Woman: It's out of order.

Question　What does the woman mean?

(男)：その機械はどうして動かないんだろう。

(女)：それは故障しているわ。

質問　女性は何と言っていますか。

16.　解答：B

解説　keep an eye on は「見張る」の意味で，男性は女性のスーツケースを見張ると言っている。B が正解。

A. 彼は彼女のスーツケースの写真を撮るだろう。

B. 彼は彼女のスーツケースを見張るだろう。

C. 彼は彼女のスーツケースを人にやるだろう。

D. 彼は彼女のスーツケースを盗むだろう。

ナレーション

Woman: I need to get a ticket for the bus.

Man:　　I'll keep an eye on your suitcase.

Question　What does the man mean?

(女)：バスの切符を買わなくちゃならないわ。

(男)：僕があなたのスーツケースを見張っておきましょう。

質問　男性は何と言っていますか。

17.　解答：D

解説　replace は「～を…と取り替える」の意味で，女性は男性の壊れたコーヒーカップを新しいコーヒーカップと取り替えると言っている。D が正解。

A. 彼女は彼のコーヒーカップを探すでしょう。

B. 彼女は彼とコーヒーを飲むでしょう。

C. 彼女は彼にコーヒーを淹《い》れるでしょう。

D. 彼女は彼に新しいコーヒーカップをあげるでしょう。

ナレーション

Man:　　My coffee cup is broken.

Woman: I'll replace it.

Question　What does the woman mean?

(男)：僕のコーヒーカップは壊れているんだ。

(女)：新しいコーヒーカップと取り替えましょう。

質問　女性は何と言っていますか。

18.　解答：A

解説 extraordinaryは「並はずれた」の意味で，男性は彼女が素晴らしいピアニストだと言っている。Aが正解。

A. 彼女は素晴らしいピアニストだ。

B. 彼女はピアノが弾けない。

C. 彼女は下手なピアニストではない。

D. 彼女はいつか立派なピアニストになるかもしれない。

ナレーション

Woman: She plays the piano very well.

Man:　She's an extraordinary pianist.

Question　What does the man mean?

(女)：彼女はピアノがとても上手だわ。

(男)：彼女は驚異的なピアニストだね。

質問　男性は何と言っていますか。

19.　解答：C

解説 女性は男性に医者に診てもらうべきだと言っている。Cが正解。

A. 彼は医者に診てもらうべきではない。　B. 彼は医者を手伝うべきだ。

C. 彼は医者に診てもらうべきだ。　D. 彼は医者を避けるべきだ。

ナレーション

Man:　I think there's something wrong with my stomach.

Woman: You should consult with your doctor.

Question　What does the woman mean?

(男)：僕の胃の調子が悪いと思うんだ。

(女)：医者に相談しなくちゃ。

質問　女性は何と言っていますか。

20.　解答：C

解説 put upは「…を泊める」の意味で，男性は，女性の家族が男性を泊めてくれたことに感謝していると言っている。Cが正解。

A. 彼は彼の友達が彼を訪れるのがうれしい。

B. 彼は彼女の家族が彼と一緒に滞在したことがうれしい。

C. 彼は彼女の家族が彼を泊めてくれたことに感謝している。

D. 彼は彼女の家族が彼を訪れたことに驚いている。

ナレーション

Woman: It's been great to have you with my family.

Man: Thank you for putting me up.

Question What does the man mean?

(女)：あなたが私の家族と過ごせてよかったわ。

(男)：僕を泊めてくれてありがとう。

質問 男性は何と言っていますか。

III まとまりのある内容の英文（300語前後）を2度聴いたあと，その内容に関する英語の質問を聴いて答えるリスニングテスト。10問出題。

21. 解答：D

解説 "I met him forty years ago when I was a senior at a university." から，正解はD。

A. 6年前 B. 10年前 C. 30年前 D. 40年前

22. 解答：B

解説 "We both majored in English literature" から，正解はB。

A. 日本文学 B. 英文学 C. 英会話 D. アメリカ史

23. 解答：A

解説 "I met him forty years ago when I was a senior at a university." から，正解はA。

A. 大学で B. 高等学校で

C. クラブ活動で D. ライティングの授業で

24. 解答：B

解説 "At the beginning of our fourth-year seminar, the teacher told us to write about what we wanted to do in the future." から，正解は B。

A. もっと一生懸命に勉強すること　B. 将来について考えること

C. 早く卒業すること　D. 大学院に進むこと

25. 解答：D

解説 "I wanted to go on to graduate school and to become a professor." から，正解は D。

A. 作家になること　B. 彼女のクラスメートと知り合いになること

C. 日本文学を専攻すること　D. 教授になること

26. 解答：B

解説 "I never expected to experience such bitterness so early in life." から，正解は B。

A. 彼女は理解できなかった。　B. 彼女はとても失望した。

C. 彼女は気にしなかった。　D. 彼女は作家になろうと考えを変えた。

27. 解答：A

解説 "Whenever I start losing hope, there is one thing I always do. I keep doing things that I truly love to do." から，正解は A。

A. 彼女のやりたいことをやり続けること

B. 彼女のやりたいことを諦めること

C. 彼女の将来のためにお金を貯めること

D. 彼女の日記をつけること

28. 解答：C

解説 "Thanks to Ken's advice, I was accepted by a graduate school in America." から，正解は C。

A. 彼女は会社の試験に合格した。

B. 彼女は日本の大学に入学した。

C. 彼女はアメリカの大学院に入学した。

D. 彼女は日本の大学の奨学金をもらった。

29. 解答：A

解説 “Unfortunately, I lost track of him because I was so busy with my graduate work in America.” から，正解は A。

A. 彼女はアメリカでの大学の研究でとても忙しくなった。
B. 彼女は彼のことを単に忘れてしまった。
C. 彼女は彼をつまらないと思った。
D. 彼女は彼が彼女を嫌いだと思った。

30. 解答：A

解説 “He was finally recognized as a great writer at the age of 62.” から，正解は A。

A. 彼は偉大な作家になった。　B. 彼は教授になった。
C. 彼は希望を失った。　D. 彼はアメリカに行った。

ナレーション

My name is Keiko. Let me tell you a story about my long-lost friend. His name is Ken. I met him forty years ago when I was a senior at a university. We both majored in English literature and were in the same fourth-year seminar. Whenever I saw him, he was always writing in his small notebook.

At the beginning of our fourth-year seminar, the teacher told us to write about what we wanted to do in the future. I wanted to go on to graduate school and to become a professor. There was only one graduate student accepted at our university that year and that person was not me. I failed the exam. I never expected to experience such bitterness so early in life.

Seeing my disappointment, Ken talked to me for the first time. He said, “I understand how you’re feeling, Keiko. It may seem life is treating you unfairly. I’ve been in your position a few times. Whenever I start losing hope, there is one thing I always do. I keep doing things that I truly love to do. In my case, I want to be a good writer. That’s why I practice writing every day, hoping I will be recognized as a published writer someday.”

Thanks to Ken's advice, I was accepted by a graduate school in America. I even got a scholarship for my work. After I got my graduate degree in English literature, a university in Japan hired me and eventually I became a full professor. I owe Ken so much for what I am. Unfortunately, I lost track of him because I was so busy with my graduate work in America.

One day I was reading a newspaper and came across an article about a writer who was awarded a major writing prize. At last, I found my long-lost friend. He kept writing even when things didn't work well for him. He was finally recognized as a great writer at the age of 62.

Questions 21. When did Keiko meet Ken?
22. What was Keiko's major?
23. Where did Keiko meet Ken?
24. What did Keiko's seminar teacher tell the students to do?
25. What did Keiko want to do after finishing university?
26. How was Keiko feeling when she failed the exam for her university's graduate school?
27. What was Ken's advice to Keiko?
28. What happened to Keiko after following Ken's advice?
29. Why did Keiko lose track of Ken?
30. What became of Ken?

訳例　私の名前はケイコです。長い間音信不通だった友人についてお話しましょう。彼の名前はケンです。40年前，私が大学４年生だったとき彼に会いました。私たちは両方とも英文学を専攻し，同じ４年生ゼミに入っていました。私が彼に会うといつも彼は小さなノートに書いていました。

４年生ゼミの最初に，先生は私たちが将来やりたいことについて書くように言いました。私は大学院に入って大学の先生になりたかったのです。私たちの大学ではその年１名だけ大学院に入学ができましたが，それは私ではありませんでした。私は試験に落ちたのです。私は人生の早い時期にこんな辛さを経験するとは思ってもいませんでした。

私が失望しているのを見たケンは，初めて私に話しかけたのです。「あなたの気持ちがわかります，ケイコ。人生は不公平だと思っているかもしれません。僕はそんな経験を2，3回しました。希望を失いかけたとき必ず僕がしていることが1つあります。僕が本当にやりたいことをやり続けることです。僕の場合，立派な作家になりたいのです。だから，いつか名の知れた作家になれると思って毎日書く練習をしているのです。」

ケンのアドバイスのおかげで私はアメリカの大学院に合格しました。研究の奨学金までもらえました。英文学の学位を大学院で取得した後，日本の大学が私を採用し，最終的に正教授になりました。私がいまあるのはケンのおかげです。残念なことに，アメリカでの大学院の勉強で忙しかったので彼への連絡が途絶えてしまいました。

ある日新聞を読んでいると，ある作家が主要な文学賞を受賞したという記事を見つけました。ついに私は懐かしい友人を見つけたのでした。彼は物事がうまくいかないときも書き続けました。62歳でやっと彼は偉大な作家として認められたのでした。

質問　21. ケイコはいつケンに会いましたか。
22. ケイコの専攻は何でしたか。
23. ケイコはどこでケンに会いましたか。
24. ケイコのゼミの先生は学生に何をするように言いましたか。
25. ケイコは大学卒業後，何になりたかったのですか。
26. 大学院への試験に合格しなかったときケイコはどんな気持ちでしたか。
27. ケンのケイコへのアドバイスは何でしたか。
28. ケンのアドバイスのとおりにするとケイコにどんなことが起きましたか。
29. ケイコはなぜケンとの連絡が途絶えてしまったのですか。
30. ケンはどうなったのですか。

IV

会話を2度聴いたあと，
その内容に関する英語の質問を聴いて答えるリスニングテスト。10問出題。

31.　解答：C

解説　オンライン授業についてメグは，学生が質問をすることと，プレゼンテーションが上達するという肯定的な点と，個々の学生の評価が大人数オンライン授業では困難な点を述べていることから，正解はC。

A. 彼女は優柔不断だ。

B. 彼女は答えたくない。

C. 彼女は２つの正反対の意見を持っている。
D. 彼女はジムの質問が理解できなかった。

32.　解答：A

解説　メグが “The positive things about online classes are that students tend to ask many questions ...” と言っていることから，正解は A。

A. 学生はたくさんの質問をする。
B. 先生は簡単に学生の出席をチェックできる。
C. 学生はチャット機能を使わない。
D. 先生は学生にたくさん勉強させることができる。

33.　解答：B

解説　ジムが “They seem more motivated in online classes.” と言っていることから，正解は B。

A. 彼は，オンライン授業は管理が難しいと感じている。
B. 彼は学生の意欲がもっと上がっていると感じている。
C. 彼はオンライン授業を体験したいと思っている。
D. 彼はチャット機能を使いたいと思っている。

34.　解答：C

解説　メグが “Another good point is that they become good at presentation. They present their assignments using slides and share them in the class.” と言っていることから，正解は C。

A. 学生の意見を交わさないこと
B. 写真を撮ること
C. スライドを用いて課題を発表すること
D. 他の学生に課題を出すこと

35.　解答：A

解説　メグが “They have worked hard at how to do presentations online, both in presenting their material and maintaining the quality of their work.” と言っていることから，正解は A。

A. 学修の質　　B. 学修の量

C. 共有できる量　D. 締切に間に合わせること

36. 解答：D

解説　ジムがメグにオンライン授業での大人数の場合の人数を "How about a large-sized online class with 50 or more students?" と設定して尋ねていることから，正解は D。

A. 約 20 人　B. 約 30 人
C. 約 40 人　D. 約 50 人または 50 人以上

37. 解答：B

解説　メグが "But, it is hard to evaluate students' accomplishment individually." と言っていることから，正解は B。

A. 学生の名前を覚えること　B. 学生の成果を個々に評価すること
C. 学生に課題を出すこと　D. 学生の課題を集めること

38. 解答：A

解説　ジムがメグに "You may want to give them a comprehension test during a class hour." と提案していることから，正解は A。

A. 学生に理解度のテストをする　B. 補講をする
C. 発表をする　D. 学生に講義をする

39. 解答：C

解説　メグはジムに "Let me try it next time when I teach a large class online." と言っていることから，正解は C。

A. 彼女はそれが役に立つとは思わない。
B. 彼女はジムがそれを試してみるべきだと思っている。
C. 彼女はそれを試すつもりだ。
D. 彼女は何か別のことを考えるだろう。

40. 解答：D

解説　ジムとメグの会話にはメグの教えている分野について述べられていないことから，正解は D。

A. 英語　B. 写真　C. 看護　D. それは述べられていない

ナレーション

Jim: As a teacher, do you like online classes, Meg?

Meg: Yes and no, Jim.

Jim: Could you tell me why?

Meg: The positive things about online classes are that students tend to ask many questions and that they discuss issues through the chat function. Students don't usually ask many questions in the ordinary classroom.

Jim: That's interesting. They seem more motivated in online classes.

Meg: Another good point is that they become good at presentation. They present their assignments using slides and share them in the class.

Jim: Wow! How do they get presentation skills in an online class?

Meg: They have worked hard at how to do presentations online, both in presenting their material and maintaining the quality of their work.

Jim: It sounds great for a small-sized class. How about a large-sized online class with 50 or more students?

Meg: That's a problem I wanted to talk about. If a class does not require teacher and student interaction, a large-sized online class may be all right. But, it is hard to evaluate students' accomplishment individually.

Jim: I have a suggestion for that. You may want to give them a comprehension test during a class hour.

Meg: Thank you for your advice! Let me try it next time when I teach a large class online.

Questions 31. Why does Meg answer, "Yes and no" to Jim's question?

32. What is one of the good points about online classes according to Meg?

33. How does Jim feel about online classes after hearing Meg's online class experiences?

34. What else have students become good at through

online classes?

35. What is one thing students worked hard at when they gave presentations in an online class?
36. About how many students are there in a large class according to the conversation?
37. What does Meg say is difficult for a large online class?
38. What is Jim's suggestion for a large online class?
39. What does Meg say to Jim's suggestion for a large online class?
40. What does Meg teach?

訳例　ジム：教師としてオンライン授業は好きかい，メグ。
メグ：イエスとも言えるしノーとも言えるわ，ジム。
ジム：その理由をおしえてくれる？
メグ：オンライン授業のいいところは，学生がたくさんの質問をする傾向があることと，チャット機能を使って問題を議論することね。普通の教室では，学生はあまり質問しないの。
ジム：それは興味深いね。学生はオンライン授業の方がもっと意欲があるようだね。
メグ：もう1ついい点は，プレゼンテーションが上手になることよ。授業で課題をスライドで発表しそれをクラスで共有するの。
ジム：すごいね。オンライン授業で学生はどうやって発表のスキルを身に付けるの？
メグ：学生は資料の発表の仕方や学修の質を維持できるように，オンラインでの発表方法を一生懸命に学んだの。
ジム：少人数の授業にはよさそうだね。50人とかそれ以上の学生がいる大人数のオンライン授業の場合はどうなの？
メグ：それが私の話したかった問題点なの。先生と学生の相互作用が必要のない授業なら大人数のオンライン授業でもいいかもしれないわ。でも，学生の成果を個別に評価するのは難しいわ。
ジム：それについて僕は提案があるよ。授業中に理解力テストをしたらどうだろう。
メグ：アドバイス，ありがとう。今度，オンラインで大人数のクラスを教えるときに試してみるわ。

質問　31. なぜメグは，ジムの質問に対して“Yes and no”と答えているのですか。
32. メグによるとオンライン授業のいい点の1つは何ですか。

33. メグのオンライン授業の経験を聞いて，ジムはオンライン授業についてどのように感じていますか。
34. オンライン授業を通して学生が上達したことは他に何がありますか。
35. オンライン授業で発表をするときに学生が頑張ったことの1つは何ですか。
36. 会話によると，大人数の授業には何人くらいの学生がいますか。
37. メグは，大人数のオンライン授業の難しい点は何だと言っていますか。
38. ジムは大人数のオンライン授業のために何を提案していますか。
39. 大人数のオンライン授業に関するジムの提案に対してメグは何と言っていますか。
40. メグは何を教えていますか。

V

英文の下線部の意味を最もよく表す語または語句を4つの選択肢中から1つ選ぶ問題。10問出題。

41. 解答：B

解説 gold は「親切な，美しい，寛大な」の意味なので，B が正解。

訳例 彼女は親切な心の持ち主だ。

A. 輝いている　B. 親切だ

C. たくさんの金をもっている　D. 冷たい心を持っている

42. 解答：D

解説 be hard hit は「大打撃を受ける」の意味なので，D が正解。

訳例 パンデミックの間ビジネスは大打撃を受けた。

A. 記録を作った　B. ヒットした

C. 同じままだった　D. 痛手をこうむった

43. 解答：C

解説 go for nothing は「水泡に帰する」の意味なので，C が正解。

訳例 彼の努力は無駄になった。

A. 何かの役に立った　B. 面白かった
C. 無駄だった　D. 有名になった

44. 解答：D

解説　hand in は「提出する」の意味だから，D が正解。

訳例　あなたは明日課題を提出しなければなりません。
A. 手書きをする　B. 写す　C. 話し合う　D. 提出する

45. 解答：C

解説　like talking to a wall は「壁に向かって話しているようで」の意味なので，C が正解。

訳例　彼と話すことは，壁に向かって話しているようだった。
A. 必要な　B. 有益な　C. 役に立たない　D. 価値がある

46. 解答：A

解説　walk away from は「逃げる，関わり合いになるのを避ける」の意味なので，A が正解。

訳例　彼女は難しい仕事から逃げた。
A. 断念した　B. 計画した　C. 要求した　D. 実験した

47. 解答：B

解説　take five は「5 分間休む，小休止する」の意味なので，B が正解。

訳例　休憩しましょう。
A. 行く　B. 休憩する　C. 仕事に取りかかる　D. 5 時まで働く

48. 解答：D

解説　bunch は「束」，a whole bunch of で「ものすごい数の」の意味なので，D が正解。

訳例　彼は彼女にたくさんの花をあげた。
A. いくつかの新鮮な　B. 2，3 の
C. いくつかの鮮やかな　D. たくさんの

49. 解答：A

解説　keep up appearances は「体裁を繕う，対面を保つ」の意味なので，A

が正解。

訳例　彼女はいつも体裁をつくろっています。

A. ふりをしている　B. 彼女の家族を訪れている

C. 真実を言っている　D. 上手に歌っている

50.　解答：D

解説　dispose of は「を処分する」の意味なので，D が正解。

訳例　ゴミを捨ててくださいますか。

A. 軽減する　B. 凍らせる　C. 一列に並べる　D. 取り除く

VI

300～400 語程度のまとまりのある文を国連英検指定テキスト『新 わかりやすい国連の活動と世界』から抜粋し，その内容を把握しているかどうかを問う問題。10 題出題。

51.　解答：C

解説　"The General Assembly has no power to compel any government to take any action." から，C が正解。

訳例　総会は各国政府に対して何を強制しないのですか。

A. 互いに協力すること　B. 平和を維持すること

C. 行動を取ること　D. 互いを無視すること

52.　解答：B

解説　"The General Assembly may discuss any issue coming within the scope of the Charter of the United Nations" から，B が正解。

訳例　総会はどのような問題について審議しますか。

A. 国連憲章の範囲外の問題　B. 国連憲章の範囲内の問題

C. 国連組織に関係ない問題　D. 特定の政府に関する問題

53.　解答：A

解説　"It may discuss any issue concerning peace and security that is brought before it by a Member State," から，A が正解。

訳例　平和と安全に関する問題を審議するよう総会に提起する組織の 1 つはどれですか。

A. 加盟国　B. いかなる政府でも

C. 世界で非常に重要な国々　D. 世界貿易機関

54. 解答：A

解説 “It [The General Assembly] also examines the administrative budgets of the specialized agencies.” から，A が正解。

訳例 どの組織が専門機関の運営予算の審査をしますか。
A. 総会　B. 安全保障理事会　C. 経済社会理事会　D. 信託統治理事会

55. 解答：C

解説 “Special sessions may be called at the request of the Security Council, of a majority of Member States, as well as at the request of one Member State with the concurrence of a majority.” から，C が正解。

訳例 本文の内容に合わないものはどれですか。
A. 総会は毎年 1 回定期的に開催される。
B. 定例会議は翌年に再開されることもある。
C. 特別総会はいかなる時も招集されない。
D. 緊急特別総会は 24 時間以内に招集される。

56. 解答：B

解説 exercise は「(権力・権利など) を行使する」の意味だから，B が正解。

訳例 下線部 (56) exercised の意味は何ですか。
A. について話した　B. 行使した　C. 取り上げた　D. 除外した

57. 解答：C

解説 scope は「範囲」の意味だから，C が正解。

訳例 下線部 (57) scope の意味は何ですか。
A. ガラス　B. 観察　C. 範囲　D. 調査

58. 解答：A

解説 body は「機関」の意味だから，A が正解。

訳例 下線部 (58) body の意味は何ですか。
A. 機関　B. 姿　C. 負担　D. 交渉

59. 解答：C

解説 dispute は「論争，紛争」の意味だから，C が正解。

訳例　下線部 (59) dispute の意味は何ですか。

A. 利益　B. 返答　C. 論争　D. 分類

60. 解答：D

解説　settlement は「合意，解決」の意味だから，D が正解。

訳例　下線部 (60) settlement の意味は何ですか。

A. 無知　B. 公式　C. 展示　D. 同意

訳例　総会は，各国政府に対していかなる行動も強制する権限を持たない。その影響力は，世界の世論の総意としての勧告という形で行使される。

総会は，国連憲章の範囲内の問題，もしくは憲章の下に設置された国連機関に関する問題について審議し，加盟国あるいは安全保障理事会，あるいはその双方に勧告する。ただし，安全保障理事会が現に審議中の紛争もしくは事態については，安全保障理事会から要請がない限り勧告しない。

総会は，平和と安全を維持するための協力の原則を審議する。その中には軍縮および軍備規制を管理する原則も含まれる。総会は，加盟国，安全保障理事会，もしくは事前に国連憲章にある平和的解決の義務を受け入れた非加盟国から提起された平和と安全に関する問題について審議し，その問題が安全保障理事会で現に審議中である場合を除き，当該国家もしくは関連諸国家あるいは安全保障理事会，もしくはその双方に勧告を行う。

国連の財政は総会が管理し，通常予算を承認し，加盟各国への分配金を割り当てる。また総会は，専門機関の運営予算の審査を行う。

総会の定例会議は毎年 9 月の第 3 火曜日に始まり，12 月半ばまで続く。定例会議は，場合によって翌年に再開されることもある。特別総会は，安全保障理事会もしくは加盟国の過半数，もしくは過半数の同意を得た 1 加盟国の要請によって招集される。緊急特別総会は，9 理事国の賛成を得た安全保障理事会もしくは加盟国の過半数の要請により，24 時間以内に招集される。

『新 わかりやすい国連の活動と世界』pp. 54–55

VII

2 つの文章に共通して用いられる語を 1 つ，選択肢の中から選ぶ問題。
10 問出題。

61. 解答：B

解説　broke は break の過去形，他動詞で「(記録を) 破る，更新する」，形容詞で go broke は「文なしになる，破産する」の意味。正解は B。

訳例　「彼女はランニングで学校の記録を破りました」
「彼は中古車販売に失敗して破産した」

A. 失った　C. 家　D. 下へ

62. 解答：D

解説 loafは名詞で「パン1塊」，自動詞で「だらだら過ごす」の意味。正解はD。

訳例 「私は1斤のパンが必要です」
「彼はきょう，だらだらと過ごしたい」
A. ゆっくり走る　B. 頭　C. 働く

63. 解答：A

解説 breakは名詞で「休憩」「割れ目，裂け目」の意味。正解はA。

訳例 「そのジャズの演奏家たちはしばらく休憩した」
「壁にいくつか割れ目がある」
B. 休息　C. 飲み物　D. スナック

64. 解答：B

解説 forceは他動詞で「強制する」，名詞で「(物理的な）力，強さ」の意味。正解はB。

訳例 「彼らは無理やり彼らのやり方を強制した」
「地球の重力の力は適度です」
A. 押す　C. 飛ぶ　D. 固定する

65. 解答：A

解説 drawは他動詞で「引き出す」，名詞で「引き分け」の意味。正解はA。

訳例 「私はお金をおろさなければなりません」
「テニスの試合は引き分けでした」
B. 節約する　C. 引き分け　D. 夢

66. 解答：C

解説 completeは他動詞で「(必要事項を）記入する」，形容詞で「(機関などが）まるまる」の意味。正解はC。

訳例 「用紙に必要事項を記入してください」
「私がその仕事を終えるのに丸1年が必要だった」
A. 満たす　B. 余分の　D. 加える

67. 解答：B

解説 forward は他動詞で「転送する」，副詞で「早めて」の意味。正解は B。

訳例 「彼女にこの伝言を転送してくださいますか」

「私は時計を早めなければなりません」

A. 送る　C. 添付する　D. 費やす

68. 解答：A

解説 express は他動詞で「表現する」，名詞で「急行」の意味。正解は A。

訳例 「彼女は感謝を表すスピーチをした」

「私は急行列車に乗った」

B. 紹介する　C. 述べる　D. 速い

69. 解答：B

解説 shelter は他動詞で「保護する」，名詞で「住居」の意味。正解は B。

訳例 「彼女は迷った犬を保護したかった」

「衣食住は私たちの必需品です」

A. 保護する　C. 家具　D. 住宅

70. 解答：D

解説 post は他動詞で「掲載する」，名詞で「職」の意味。正解は D。

訳例 「その作家は自分のエッセイを自身のウェブサイトに掲載するのが好きです」

「彼女はその会社の職に就いた」

A. 書く　B. 仕事　C. 保つ

VIII 4つの文章の中で，文法的に用法が間違っているものを見つける問題。10問出題。

71. 解答：B

Let go the rope. → Let go of the rope.

「ロープを手から離しなさい」

解説 go の用法を問う問題。A の to go は「持ち帰りの」，C の go over は「読み返す」，D の go without は「なしですます」の意味。B は let go of で「を離す」の意味なので，Let go the rope. ではなく Let go of the rope. が正しい。B が正解。

訳例 A. このコーヒーをここで召し上がりますか，それともお持ち帰りされますか。

C. その報告書を読み返してくださいますか。
D. 私は1週間インターネットなしで過ごさなければならなかった。

72. 解答：D

around clock → around the clock

「その店は24時間営業している」

解説 clockの用法を問う問題。Aのset the alarm clockは「目覚まし時計をセットする」，Bのagainst the clockは「時間に追われて」，Cのbeat the clockは「定刻以前に仕事を終える」の意味。Dはaround the clockで「24時間ぶっ通しで」の意味なので，around clockではなくaround the clockが正しい。Dが正解。

訳例 A. 私は目覚まし時計を7時にセットした。
B. 彼は時間に追われて仕事をしなければならなかった。
C. 彼女はいつも定時前に仕事を終える。

73. 解答：A

is back on business → is back in business

「そのレストランは営業を再開しています」

解説 businessの用法を問う問題。Bのget down to businessは「まじめに（本腰を入れて）仕事に取り掛かる」，Cのhave no business ...ingは「…する権利はない」，Dのout of businessは「倒産して」の意味。Aはis back in businessで「事業を再開する」の意味なので，is back on businessではなくis back in businessが正しい。Aが正解。

訳例 B. 彼は休暇の後本腰を入れて仕事にとりかかった。
C. 彼女はあなたに何をすべきかを言う権利はありません。
D. そのホテルは昨年倒産した。

74. 解答：C

in her own account → on her own account

「彼女は独力で能力があります」

解説 accountの用法を問う問題。Aのopen an accountは「口座を開設する」，Bのon my accountは「私のことを思って」，Dのdo the accountsは「帳簿をつける」の意味。Cはon one's own accountで「独りで，独力で」の意味なので，in her own account ではなく on her own account が正しい。C が正解。

訳例　A. 私は銀行で口座を開かなければなりません。
B. 私のことを思って心配しないでください。
D. 彼は会社で帳簿をつけます。

75.　解答：B

took in his bed → took to his bed

「彼は晩年病床についた」

解説　bed の用法を問う問題。A の put O to bed は「(子供など) を寝かしつける」，C の a bed of nails は「針のむしろ，地獄」，D の go to bed は「寝る」の意味。B は take to one's bed で「病床につく」の意味なので，took in his bed ではなく took to his bed が正しい。B が正解。

訳例　A. 彼女は子供たちを 9 時に寝かしつけなければならない。
C. 状況は針のむしろのようだった。
D. 寝る時間です。

76.　解答：A

on the board → on board

「どうかフェリーボートにご乗船ください」

解説　board の用法を問う問題。B の cutting board は「まな板」，C の board は「重役会，役員会」，D の board up は「板でふさぐ」の意味。B は on board で「(船・飛行機・列車・バスなど) に乗って」の意味なので，on the board ではなく on board が正しい。A が正解。

訳例　B. 彼は玉ねぎをまな板に置いた。
C. 彼女は重役です。
D. 私は嵐のため板で窓を塞がなければなりません。

77.　解答：D

Bottom up! → Bottoms up!

「乾杯！」

解説　bottom の用法を問う問題。A の get to the bottom of は「…の真相を突き止める」，B の from the bottom of one's heart は「心の底から」，C の at the bottom of the form は「書式のいちばん下に」の意味。D は

Bottoms up! で「乾杯！」の意味なので，Bottom up! ではなく Bottoms up! が正しい。D が正解。

訳例　A. その問題の真相を突き止めましょう。
B. 彼は人々に心の底から感謝した。
C. 書式のいちばん下にあなたの住所を書いてください。

78. 解答：B

burnt the midnight oils → burnt the midnight oil

「彼は夜遅くまで勉強した」

解説　oil の用法を問う問題。A の oil painting は「油絵」，C の oil and water は「水と油のように合わない」，D の pour oil on troubled water は「けんかを穏便に収める，仲裁する」の意味。B は burnt the midnight oil で「夜遅くまで勉強する」の意味なので，burnt the midnight oils ではなく burnt the midnight oil が正しい。B が正解。

訳例　A. 彼は油絵が上手い。
C. 彼らは水と油のように合わない。
D. けんかを仲裁してはいけません。

79. 解答：C

passed away → passed up

「彼女は宴会への招待を断った」

解説　pass の用法を問う問題。A の pass on は「伝える」，B の pass out は「意識を失う」，D の pass away は「死ぬ」の意味。C は pass up で「（招待など）を断る」の意味なので，passed away ではなく passed up が正しい。C が正解。

訳例　A. その情報をあなたの友達に伝えてください。
B. 彼は会議中に意識を失った。
D. その有名な歌手は自然死した。

80. 解答：D

Most of students → Most of the students

「学生のほとんどは教室にいた」

解説　most の用法を問う問題。A の make the most of は「を最大限に活かす」，B の most of all は「とりわけ」，C の at most は「せいぜい」の意味。D は most of the students で「ほとんどの学生」の意味なので，most of students ではなく most of the students が正しい。D が正解。

訳例 A. 彼女は時間を最大限に活かした。

B. 彼はとりわけ推理小説を読むことが好きです。

C. それはせいぜい 2 時間しかかからないだろう。

IX

300 語前後のまとまりのある文を読み，読解力を試す問題。
空所補充，語句の並べ替え，語彙力，行間を読む力を問う問題を 10 問出題。

81. 解答：D

解説 The American space agency has successfully landed its Perseverance Mars rover on the surface of Mars ... から，D が正解。

訳例 "Touchdown confirmed: There's a new robot on the surface of Mars." これはどんな意味ですか。

A. 探査車パーシビアランスは火星に不時着した。

B. 探査車パーシビアランスは火星から外の宇宙に飛び立った。

C. 探査車パーシビアランスは火星に着陸し地球へ戻ってきた。

D. 探査車パーシビアランスは火星のクレーターに無事着陸した。

82. 解答：C

解説 "The American space agency has successfully landed its Perseverance Mars rover on the surface of Mars in a deep crater near the planet's equator called Jezero." から，C が正解。

訳例 "Jezero" とは何ですか。

A. 南カリフォルニアにあるアメリカ宇宙機関本部

B. 探査車パーシビアランスの名前

C. 探査車パーシビアランスが着陸したクレーターの名前

D. クレーターに住む動物

83. 解答：B

解説 "The six-wheeled vehicle will now spend at least the next two years drilling into the local rocks" から，B が正解。

訳例 何年間 6 輪車の火星探査車は岩を掘削する予定ですか。

A. 1 年間　　B. 2 年間　　C. 10 年間　　D. 永遠に

84. 解答：A

解説 “The six-wheeled vehicle will now spend at least the next two years drilling into the local rocks, looking for evidence of past life.” から，Aが正解。

訳例 探査車はジェゼロクレーターで今後2年間に何を探すのですか。
A. 数十億年前の古代生命の痕跡　B. 火星での今日の郊外生活の痕跡
C. 金，ダイアモンド，油田の痕跡　D. 上記全て

85. 解答：A

解説 “Jezero is thought to have held a giant lake billions of years ago.” から，Aが正解。

訳例 クレーターには数十億年前に何があったと考えられますか。
A. 湖　B. 砂漠　C. 雪　D. 人々

86. 解答：C

解説 “In the past they might have hugged or *high-fived but strict coronavirus *protocols meant they had all been separated by *Perspex screens.” から，Cが正解。

訳例 アメリカの宇宙機関の関係者は探査車の着陸にどのように反応しましたか。
A. 彼らはとても失望した。
B. 彼らは互いに抱き合い，「ハイタッチ」をした。
C. 新型コロナウイルス感染症のため彼らは感情を抑え，アクリル板で隔てられていた。
D. 彼らは酔っ払い火星パーティーをした。

87. 解答：B

解説 “it was possible to see a flat surface both in front and behind the rover” から，Bが正解。

訳例 アメリカ宇宙機関の関係者は火星の表面で最初に何がはっきり見えましたか。
A. 何も見えなかった　B. 探査車の前後の景色　C. 湖　D. 火星人

88. 解答：B

解説 “The vehicle is only *tilted by about 1.2 degrees,” “So we did successfully find that parking lot and have a safe rover on the ground.” から，B が正解。

訳例　アレン・チェンは “I couldn’t be more proud of my team doing that.” と述べました。彼は何を言いたかったのですか。

A. 彼は火星に行くのを楽しんだ。

B. 大変困難だったがチームはわずかな傾きだけで火星探査車を完璧に着陸させた。

C. ミッションすべてが失敗に終わったとき，チームはとても勇敢だった。

D. 幸運にもチームの誰かが火星の人々と通信することができた。

89.　解答：A

解説　“In the past they might have hugged or high-fived but strict coronavirus protocols meant they had all been separated by Perspex screens. A *respectful fist bump was about all they could manage.” から，チームが互いにより注意したことがわかる。A が正解。

訳例　スティーブ・ジャーチェックは新型コロナウイルス感染症に関する困難について何と言っていますか。

A. 火星着陸船に注意を払いながら，互いになおさら注意すること。

B. 火星着陸船だけに注意すること。

C. チームだけに注意すること。

D. 火星の人々に新型コロナウイルス感染症をうつさないようにすること。

90.　解答：C

解説　“Touchdown confirmed: There’s a new robot on the surface of Mars” から，C が正解。

訳例　この話のタイトルに最もふさわしいものはどれですか。

A. 火星着陸船の失敗　　B. 火星に一緒に行こう

C. 難関の中での，火星着陸船の成功　　D. 火星着陸船，月に行く

訳例　「着陸確認，火星表面に新しいロボットがいます」

アメリカ宇宙機関は火星探査車パーシビアランスをジェゼロと呼ばれる火星の赤道近くの深いクレーターに着陸させることに成功した。

ミッションの副プロジェクトマネージャーのマット・ウォレスは「宇宙船が素晴らしい状態にあるのはいい知らせです」と言った。

カリフォルニアにある NASA（アメリカ宇宙局）ミッションコントロールのエンジニアたちは，着陸が確認されたとき喜びの声を上げた。

６輪車の探査車は，過去の生命の痕跡を探して，少なくとも今後２年間はそ

の地域の岩石を掘削する予定である。

ジェゼロには数十億年前に巨大な湖があったと考えられている。そして，水があった場所には，生命が存在した可能性がある。

火星探査車パーシビアランスが降りて無事に到着したことをグリニッジ標準時間 20 時 55 分に管制官に知らせる信号が送られた。過去には，彼らは抱き合ったりハイタッチしたりしていたかもしれないが，厳格なコロナウイルス感染対策により，全員がアクリル板で隔てられていた。丁重に拳を突き合わせるくらいしかできなかった。

それにもかかわらず，興奮は明らかだった。そして，最初の 2 つの画像が入ってきたとき，拍手は続いた。まだ付いている半透明のレンズカバーは，ほこりをかぶっていたが，探査車の前も後ろも平らな面であることが確認できた。

着陸後の分析では，パーシビアランスが調査を計画しているジェゼロの三角州の南東約 2 km に車両が降下したことがわかった。

着陸チームを率いたアレン・チェン氏は，「私たちは素晴らしい平らな場所にいます。車両は約 1.2 度傾いているだけです」と語った。「つまり私たちは探査車の駐車スペースを見つけることができ，探査車が無事に着陸できたのです。これを達成したチームを最高に誇りに思っています」と述べた。

NASA の長官代理であるスティーブ・ジャーチェック氏も，この功績を称え「なんと素晴らしいチームの功績でしょう。火星への探査車の着陸に伴うすべての逆境と挑戦，さらには新型コロナウイルス感染症の困難の中，まさに驚くべき成果です」と述べた。

X

まとまりのある会話文を読み，会話が行われている状況におけるイディオム，語彙力，コミュニケーションの力を試す問題。10 問出題。

91. 解答：D

解説 "Actually, this chocolate is organic and a Fairtrade product." とジェインが述べていることから，D が正解。

訳例 ジェインがボブに勧めているチョコレートの特徴の 1 つは何ですか。

A. その成分は人工的だ。

B. それは強制労働で作られた。

C. それは遺伝子組み換え食品でできていた。

D. それはフェアトレード製品だ。

92. 解答：D

解説 "Well, this is one of the marks of Fairtrade. It means this product was produced according to the Fairtrade's policies." とジェインが述

べていることから，D が正解。

訳例　消費者はどのようにしたらチョコレートがフェアトレード製品であることがわかりますか。

A. その色で　　B. 口コミで

C. 製品を食べることによって　　D. 製品のラベルに付いているマークで

93.　解答：A

解説　“the Fairtrade products are focused on ‘better prices, decent working conditions and a fairer deal for farmers and workers in developing countries’” とジェインが述べていることから，A が正解。

訳例　フェアトレードの方針の 1 つは何ですか。

A. 申し分のない労働条件　　B. 低価格

C. 雇用主のための公平な取引　　D. 不当な労働条件

94.　解答：B

解説　“There are three criteria: economic, environmental and social.” とジェインが述べていることから，B が正解。

訳例　フェアトレード製品の基準は何ですか。

A. 保険，人気，そしてイメージ　　B. 経済的，環境的，そして社会的基準

C. 創造性，研究業績，そしてテストの得点　　D. 政治信条，利益，そして量

95.　解答：A

解説　“The economic criteria include the Fairtrade Minimum Price which aims to provide producers with a safety net against falling prices” とジェインが述べていることから，A が正解。

訳例　経済的基準と違うものはどれですか。

A. フェアトレード最低価格は価格上昇に対するセーフティネットを生産者に提供することを目的とする。

B. フェアトレード最低価格は長期計画を可能にする。

C. 安定したフェアトレード・プレミアムは生産者や労働者に追加資金を供給する。

D. 安定したフェアトレード・プレミアムの追加資金はビジネスや地域社会の質向上に使うためにある。

96. 解答：C

解説 "Fairtrade prohibits the use of several hazardous materials and all genetically modified organisms (GMOs)" とジェインが述べていることから，Cが正解。

訳例 環境的基準と違うものはどれですか。
A. 適切な環境保全の実施に焦点を当てる。
B. 適切な農業の慣行に重点を置く。
C. 遺伝子組み換え品を使うことを奨励する。
D. いくつかの危険物質の使用を禁止している。

97. 解答：D

解説 "our standards require companies to operate ..., pay rates equal to or higher than the legal or regional minimum wages," とジェインが述べていることから，Dが正解。

訳例 社会的基準と違うものはどれですか。
A. 民主的自治と差別がないことが必要事項である。
B. 会社に差別のない雇用の実施を要求する。
C. 労働者の安全と健康の保護対策を会社が提供することを要求する。
D. 法律上のまたは地域の最低賃金と同等かそれ以上の賃金を企業が支払うことを許さない。

98. 解答：B

解説 "I will look for the marks next time I shop." とボブが述べていることから，Bが正解。

訳例 フェアトレードの方針を知ってボブはどのように感じていますか。
A. 彼はチョコレートに興味がなくなった。
B. 彼はフェアトレードの製品を喜んで支援しようと思っている。
C. 彼は自分と関係ないと感じている。
D. 彼はジェインが彼にもっとチョコレートを買ってくれることを期待している。

99. 解答：D

解説 "beneficial" は「有益な」の意味なので，Dが正解。

訳例 下線部 (99) beneficial の意味は何ですか。
A. 役に立たない　B. 競争的な　C. 理性的な　D. よい

100. 解答：C

解説 sound は「適切な」の意味なので，C が正解。

訳例 下線部（100）sound の意味は何ですか。
A. やかましい　B. 静かな　C. 適切な　D. できなくて

訳例 ジェイン：こんにちは，ボブ。チョコレートは好き？
ボブ：　やあ，ジェイン。うん，大好きだよ。基本的に甘いものは好きじゃないけど，チョコレートは例外なんだ。
ジェイン：このチョコレートを食べてみない？
ボブ：　いいよ，ありがとう。
ジェイン：どう？
ボブ：　こんな味，初めてだなあ。いままで食べた中でいちばんおいしいよ。どうしてこんなにおいしいんだろう。
ジェイン：実はこのチョコレートは有機でフェアトレードの商品なの。
ボブ：　「オーガニック」はわかるけど，「フェアトレード」ってどういう意味なの？
ジェイン：このマーク見たことある？
ボブ：　ないね。ラベルにこのマークが付いているのに初めて気付いたよ。
ジェイン：あのね，これはフェアトレードのマークの１つなの。つまりこの商品はフェアトレードの方針に従って生産されたことを意味しているの。
ボブ：　その方針って何なの？
ジェイン：簡単に言うと，ホームページによると，フェアトレード製品は「適正な価格，適切な労働条件，そして開発途上国の生産者や労働者の公正な取引」に焦点を当てているの。
ボブ：　それは生産者と消費者両方にとってメリットがあるようだね。
ジェイン：まさにその通りなの。フェアトレード製品を支援すれば，子供を含め，生産者や労働者を不当な労働から救うことができるの。
ボブ：　フェアトレード製品として合格する基準はどのように設定されているの？
ジェイン：経済的，環境的，社会的３つの基準があるの。
ボブ：　具体的に説明してくれる？
ジェイン：経済的基準には，フェアトレード最低価格というのがあって，生産者に価格下落に対するセーフティネットを提供し，長期的な計画を立てることができるの。それに安定したフェアトレード・プレミアムは，生産者や労働者がビジネスやコミュニティーの質を高めるために投資できる追加的な資金を提供するようになっているの。

ボブ：　環境的基準はどうなの？

ジェイン：環境的基準は，生態や農業の適切な実施に重点を置いているの。フェアトレードはいくつかの有害物質の使用やすべての遺伝子組み換作物を禁止しているわ。

ボブ：　社会的基準について教えてくれる？

ジェイン：小規模生産者のための経済的基準には，民主的な自治組織，特に協同組合や参加型の意思決定，透明性，男女同権を含む差別禁止の必要事項があるの。雇用労働が標準のプランテーション型環境では，差別のない雇用の実施，合法的な賃金あるいは地域の最低賃金に同等またはそれ以上の賃金で支払うこと，組合と労働者の団体交渉の自由，労働者の安全と健康への保護措置，労働者のフェアトレード・プレミアム管理が可能となるように会社が運営しなければならないわ。フェアトレードの基準では，強制労働や児童労働は禁止されているの。

ボブ：　フェアトレードの製品について教えてくれてありがとう。今度買い物をするときフェアトレードマークを探すことにしよう。

2021年C級第1回試験　正解一覧

I

1. C　2. A　3. B　4. C　5. D　6. B　7. A　8. B　9. C　10. D

II

11. A　12. D　13. B　14. C　15. A　16. B　17. D　18. A　19. C　20. C

III

21. D　22. B　23. A　24. B　25. D　26. B　27. A　28. C　29. A　30. A

IV

31. C　32. A　33. B　34. C　35. A　36. D　37. B　38. A　39. C　40. D

V

41. B　42. D　43. C　44. D　45. C　46. A　47. B　48. D　49. A　50. D

VI

51. C　52. B　53. A　54. A　55. C　56. B　57. C　58. A　59. C　60. D

VII

61. B　62. D　63. A　64. B　65. A　66. C　67. B　68. A　69. B　70. D

VIII

71. B　72. D　73. A　74. C　75. B　76. A　77. D　78. B　79. C　80. D

IX

81. D　82. C　83. B　84. A　85. A　86. C　87. B　88. B　89. A　90. C

X

91. D　92. D　93. A　94. B　95. A　96. C　97. D　98. B　99. D　100. C

2021年

第2回試験

問題

C級試験問題用紙

C級

外務省後援

２０２１年度第２回国際連合公用語

英語検定試験（100分）

受験上の注意

1．問題用紙は試験開始の合図があるまで開いてはいけません。その間に、この**受験上の注意を熟読しておいてください。**

2．**受験番号と氏名を解答用紙（マークシート）**に記入してください。

3．解答用紙の配布は１人１部のみです。複数の配布は致しません。

4．試験開始前は、答案への解答記入は禁止です。

5．マークシートの記入は、必ずＨＢ以上の濃い鉛筆を使って該当箇所を黒く塗りつぶしてください。書き間違いの場合は「アト」が残らないように消してください。マークシートは絶対に折ったり曲げたりしないでください。

6．受験級、受験地区、会場番号、受験番号のマークシートへの記入は監督者の指示に従い、間違いなく記入してください。**（裏表紙の「マークシート記入例」参照）**

7．試験問題についての質問は、印刷が不鮮明な場合を除き、一切受けつけません。

8．中途退室の際は、マークシートを監督者に渡し、他の受験者の迷惑にならないように静かに退室してください。中途退室後の再入室はできません。

9．試験中は他の受験者の妨げとなる行動は慎んでください。また携帯電話等の電源はお切りください。

10．マークシートは監督者に提出し、問題用紙はご自由にお持ち帰りください。

＊試験問題の複製や転載、インターネットへのアップロード等、いかなる媒体への転用を禁止します。

リスニングテストについて

1．リスニングテストは試験開始後、合図があってから実施されます。(40問あります)

2．リスニングテストが始まる前にリスニング問題の指示と内容を読んで、どういう形式のテストなのか、概要をつかんでおいてください。

3．テスト中の発言は、放送機器の具合が悪く放送された英語の聴き取りができない場合を除いて、しないようにしてください。

試験結果について

1．試験の結果は2021年11月24日㈬頃に通知します。

2．その間に住所変更をされた方は、郵便局へ住所変更の届け出を忘れずに行ってください。

3．発表前の試験結果のお問合せには応じられません。

公益財団法人　日本国際連合協会
http://www.unaj.or.jp/

Ⅰ. これから短い英文を10言います。英文は２回言います。よく聞いて、会話が成り立つように最も適切なものをA、B、C、Dの中から１つ選びなさい。途中でメモを取ってもかまいません。

1. A. That's good. B. When can I see you?
C. Don't push yourself. D. I don't know.

2. A. With pleasure. B. After you.
C. Excellent! D. Don't mention it.

3. A. I bought the glue. B. They sell locks.
C. It carries fruits. D. It's at the corner.

4. A. A diplomat. B. It's far from here.
C. No, I don't like it. D. I must work hard.

5. A. I heard the news. B. Sounds great.
C. It tastes delicious. D. I love movies.

6. A. It's near my house. B. I forgot to get my receipt.
C. Next station. D. Next Monday.

7. A. It weighs about 15 kilograms. B. It's square.
C. It has a nametag. D. It's mine.

8. A. It's terribly cold. B. Let's make it a surprise.
C. Do you have a ticket? D. I see many people in the park.

9. A. I went to college. B. I met the teacher.
C. I don't like physics. D. It's interesting.

10. A. You're late. B. You're lucky.
C. It's near the bridge. D. I paid for it.

II. これから短い会話を10言います。会話は２回繰り返します。そのあと、会話の内容について10の質問をします。質問も２回繰り返します。よく聞いて、それぞれの質問の答えとして最も適切なものをA、B、C、Dの中から１つ選びなさい。途中でメモを取ってもかまいません。

11. A. He should mind his own business.
B. She had it a fairly long time ago.
C. She had it just the other day.
D. He should stay at home.

12. A. He wants her at the wedding.
B. The woman won’t come to the wedding.
C. The man is asking her to marry him.
D. The woman will invite him to the wedding.

13. A. He’ll go to a restaurant alone.
B. She’ll make dinner.
C. She’ll invite friends for dinner.
D. They’ll go to a restaurant together.

14. A. He won’t take a day off.
B. He’ll take her home after work.
C. He’ll see a movie with her.
D. He’s very busy.

15. A. Her house needs a new roof.
B. She knows an excellent roofer.
C. He already has a roofer.
D. She thinks she needs a roofer.

16. A. He seems to like her idea.
B. He’s learning to fly.
C. He enjoys flying his plane.
D. He thinks the woman is crazy.

17. A. She’s excited.
B. She didn’t know he was married.
C. She’s not interested.
D. She’s already married.

18. A. He reads many books.
B. He reads a few books.
C. He doesn’t read at all.
D. He reads books about couples.

19. A. She’s happy because she’ll make money.
B. She’s very concerned about his safety.
C. She’s happy he is giving her a mask.
D. She doesn’t know what to do.

20. A. He's been to an art exhibition.
B. He's been at home.
C. He's seen his doctor.
D. He's been to New York.

Ⅲ. これから英文を２回繰り返します。そのあと、内容について10の質問をします。質問も２回繰り返します。よく聞いて、それぞれの質問の答えとして最も適切なものをA、B、C、Dの中から１つ選びなさい。途中でメモを取ってもかまいません。

21. A. Shopping.
B. Getting a hearing aid for George.
C. Buying a hearing aid for Yuko.
D. Shouting in George's ear.

22. A. Around 70.
B. Around 60.
C. Around 50.
D. It doesn't say.

23. A. They went by car.
B. They walked.
C. They took a train.
D. They used a bus.

24. A. Visited the ear doctor.
B. Went to department stores.
C. Bought a hearing aid that was costly and uncomfortable.
D. Went to their favorite wholesale store.

25. A. He gave George a series of tests.
B. He explained the various types of hearing aids.
C. He said the best hearing aids were rechargeable.
D. He sold George a battery-powered hearing aid.

26. A. They did not have any hearing aids.
B. Their hearing aids were expensive and not comfortable.
C. Their hearing aids were comfortable.
D. Their hearing aids were cheap.

27. A. George was given a series of hearing tests.
B. He liked the rechargeable hearing aids though they were expensive.
C. George learned his hearing aids would be adjusted for free.
D. All of the above are correct.

28. A. How comfortable the hearing aids were.
B. How cheap the hearing aids were.
C. How attractive the hearing aids were.
D. Both B and C are correct.

29. A. George could hear her once again.
B. She could go shopping.
C. She could save money.
D. She could go to the ear doctor.

30. A. Let's Go Shopping
B. The World of Ear Doctors
C. How Hearing Aids Made George and Yuko Happy
D. How to Make a Hearing Aid

Ⅳ. これから会話を２回繰り返します。そのあと、内容について10の質問をします。質問も２回繰り返します。よく聞いて、それぞれの質問の答えとして最も適切なものをA、B、C、Dの中から１つ選びなさい。途中でメモを取ってもかまいません。

31. A. It means Rika will start class.
B. Rika will discuss useful expressions in class.
C. It means to swim.
D. Rika will go home.

32. A. He's heading for the beach.
B. He wants to show his teacher he knows a "useful expression" in English.
C. He's worried the high tide is coming.
D. He feels danger.

33. A. She wants to show Jiro it involves real surfing.
B. She's afraid of the ocean.
C. She thinks Jiro's expression is formal.
D. She does not understand what "surf's up" means.

34. A. Yukio Mishima. B. Ernest Hemingway.
C. Mark Twain. D. Emily Dickinson.

35. A. He cannot pronounce "Huckleberry."
B. He believes "Finn" is the correct title of the book.
C. He believes "Finn" is more polite.
D. He believes the family name should come before the given name.

36. A. Why is your English so good?
B. Your English is a little stiff but not bad.
C. You only seem to know a few English expressions.
D. You're almost like a native speaker of English!

37. A. In English only.
B. In Japanese.
C. Equally in English and Japanese.
D. In English and German.

38. A. Critical thinking about English and American Literature.
B. Writing his feelings in English.
C. Conversations about essays in English
D. Useful expressions, grammar-translation and easy conversations.

39. A. She'll play recordings of simple English conversations.
B. She'll give lectures entirely in Japanese.
C. She'll teach short stories and poems, and have the class write about them in English.
D. She'll teach simple conversations in English.

40. A. She likes surfing and lifeguards.
B. She does not like a lifeguard's job.
C. The English learner's job is similar to that of a lifeguard.
D. It's easier for Jiro to understand English learning and what Rika is about.

V. 次の英文の下線部の意味を最もよく表す語または語句をA、B、C、Dの中から1つ選びなさい。

41. He <u>went broke</u> in Las Vegas.

A. was robbed B. got lost
C. became poor D. was staying

42. He is too careless when driving.

A. very careful B. dangerous
C. lots of fun D. good at finding places

43. Our mayor is highly estimated.

A. very rich B. calculating
C. well respected D. tall

44. He is down.

A. wealthy B. extremely happy
C. about to find something D. unhappy

45. She is a great pool player.

A. swimming pool cleaner B. carpool organizer
C. smart pool player D. fast swimmer

46. He was keyed-up before the conference.

A. nervous B. calm
C. disorganized D. humorous

47. She belongs to an academic society.

A. owns B. is a member of
C. hates D. is no longer with

48. Her publisher gave her an advance on her book.

A. money B. praise
C. information D. advice

49. I'm still coping with my problems.

A. enjoying B. forgetting
C. admiring D. dealing with

50. He is open to everyone's opinion.

A. does not care about B. does not understand
C. is indifferent to D. cares about

VI. 次の英文を読み、設問の答えとして最も適切なものをA、B、C、Dの中から1つ選びなさい。

Since 1946, the Commission on Human Rights had been the core United Nations body responsible for the promotion and protection of human rights. Whereas the Commission had made many achievements in this field through its sixty-year history, its *politicization had faced severe criticism. The 2005 World Summit, in its Outcome, *endorsed the creation of the Human Rights Council in order to further strengthen the United Nations human rights *machinery. The Commission on Human Rights was thus replaced by the Human Rights Council, which was created by the General Assembly on 15 March 2006 by its resolution 60/251. The *Sub-Commission on the Promotion and Protection of Human Rights was *likewise *superseded by the *Human Rights Council Advisory Committee.

The Human Rights Council *comprises 47 Member States elected by the General Assembly, representing a geographically fair distribution of seats. The Council members shall *pledge to contribute to the promoting and protecting of human rights. These elected members shall *uphold the highest standards in the promotion and protection of human rights.

The *Universal Periodic Review (UPR) mechanism, newly launched by the Human Rights Council, monitors and examines human rights situations in all United Nations Member States. Each year human rights situations in 42 countries are reviewed on the basis of the Charter of the United Nations, the Universal Declaration of Human Rights, Conventions to which the States are parties, voluntary *pledges made by the States and International Humanitarian Law. The Human Rights Council Advisory Committee, composed of 18 experts, serves the Human Rights Council as a think-tank advising on human rights subjects and issues. The Complaint Procedure, formerly known as the 1503 procedure, has also been established by the Council to address consistent patters of gross and reliably *attested violations of all human rights and all fundamental freedoms occurring in any part of the world and under any circumstances. The situation in question is *confidentially examined on the basis of communications submitted by the **(59)** victims of human rights violations and informal consultations with the State concerned. The Human Rights Council also works on the Special Procedures. The Council appoints special *rapporteurs, special representatives and working groups as *mandate holders, to **(60)** address specific human rights situations from a *thematic or country-specific perspective and *publicly report and advise on the situation in question.

注）*politicization　政治化　　*endorse　支持する　　*machinery　機構
*Sub-Commission on the Promotion and Protection of Human Rights　人権促進保護小委員会　　*likewise　同様に　　*supersede　に取って代わる
*Human Rights Council Advisory Committee　人権理事会諮問委員会
*comprise　を構成する　　*pledge　誓約する　　*uphold　支持する

*Universal Periodic Review 普遍的定期審査 *pledge 誓約
*attested 証拠のある *confidentially 内密に、非公開で
*rapporteur 報告者 *mandate 権限 *thematic テーマに関する
*publicly 公開で、公に

51. What are the main jobs of the Commission on Human Rights?

A. Advertisement of the General Assembly.
B. Encouragement of voluntary work.
C. The promotion and protection of human rights.
D. Advice on holding the 2005 World Summit.

52. Why was the Commission on Human Rights criticized in spite of its achievements?

A. It had political biases.
B. It fulfilled their duties well.
C. It stopped working for the United Nations.
D. It invited some politicians to the Commission.

53. Who endorsed the creation of the Human Rights Council?

A. The General Assembly in 2006.
B. The 2005 World Summit.
C. Special representatives.
D. Special rapporteurs.

54. What superseded the Sub-Commission on the Promotion and Protection of Human Rights?

A. The Commission on Human Rights.
B. The General Assembly.
C. The Human Rights Council Advisory Committee.
D. The United Nations Member States.

55. How many Member States are there in the Human Rights Council?

A. There are 42. B. There are 47.
C. There are 51. D. There are 60.

56. What shall the Council members do?

A. They shall elect Member States.
B. They shall make the Charter of the United Nations.
C. They shall become experts of geography.
D. They shall pledge to contribute to the promoting and protecting of human rights.

57. **Who monitors and examines human rights situations in all United Nations Member States?**

A. The Universal Periodic Review mechanism.
B. The Charter of the United Nations.
C. The Universal Declaration of Human Rights.
D. International Humanitarian Law.

58. **What does the Complaint Procedure deal with?**

A. Fair distribution of seats.
B. Voluntary pledges made by the States.
C. Violations of all human rights and all fundamental freedoms.
D. Promotion and Protection of the United Nations' interest.

59. **What does the underlined part (59) victims mean?**

A. violators　　B. researchers
C. sufferers　　D. employees

60. **What does the underlined part (60) address mean?**

A. choose　　B. handle
C. confirm　　D. form

Ⅶ. 次の各組の文の空所には同じ語が入ります。最も適切なものをA、B、C、Dの中から1つ選びなさい。

61. **I'll be ________ soon. Get off my ________ !**

A. head　　B. front　　C. back　　D. foot

62. **________ you help me? Put it in the garbage ________.**

A. door　　B. can　　C. will　　D. sink

63. **You need to get a ________. I got a great ________ with my new camera.**

A. shot　　B. drink　　C. car　　D. door

64. **The cat climbed over the ________. I will teach you how to________.**

A. roof　　B. wall　　C. fence　　D. shelf

65. **I am feeling ________ today. I want a ________ bicycle.**

A. yellow　　B. blue　　C. purple　　D. silver

66. **He is_________ with envy. The leaves are _________ again.**

A. green B. grey C. crazy D. orange

67. **The ship sailed in _________ weather. The election wasn't _________.**

A. rainy B. cloudy C. tropical D. fair

68. **The festival had something for _________. Not _________ needs to be famous.**

A. sale B. free C. everybody D. rocks

69. **The airplane flew on _________. You must _________ your time.**

A. water B. time C. gasoline D. schedule

70. **This website is good for _________. Oh? That's _________ to me.**

A. sports B. games C. news D. chatting

Ⅷ. 次のＡ、Ｂ、Ｃ、Ｄからなる各組の英文には下線部に誤りを含むものが１つあります。その文を選びなさい。

71. A. A cold front is coming down from Siberia.
B. There is a tall building in front of me.
C. He always sits at the front of the classroom.
D. The car in the front speeded up.

72. A. I graduated from a university in Tokyo.
B. The department store opens from 10 o'clock.
C. They moved from New York to Paris.
D. Many people died from starvation.

73. A. She did a great job.
B. He is hoping to have a full-time job.
C. The couple met at the job.
D. Nobody wants a dead-end job.

74. A. The employees will go on a strike.
B. The girl struck the last match.
C. The typhoon will strike the region.
D. He struck his foot on the door.

75. A. In short, his life was a happy one.
B. Tom is short of Thomas.
C. Could you tell me the short cut to the museum?
D. The train stopped short.

76. A. I like all student in my class.
B. All but one student went home.
C. The mother looked for her child all over the place.
D. Of all days, he had a headache on his birthday.

77. A. They discussed the root of the problem.
B. The squirrels dug up the plants by the roots.
C. I like roots vegetables.
D. We must root out bullying.

78. A. She felt small among the famous people.
B. He earns small income.
C. She answered in a small voice.
D. He loves to read till the small hours.

79. A. The magazine features an article about the scientist.
B. The new computer has special features.
C. The restaurant features seafood dishes.
D. The movie features of the actor as a famous composer.

80. A. He used some photographs in his paper for practical purposes.
B. Her purpose of going to Vienna is to study music.
C. She has a sense of purpose.
D. He did not make a mistake on the purpose.

Ⅸ. 次の英文を読み、設問の答として最も適切なものをA、B、C、Dの中から1つ選びなさい。

Facebook reported on August 11, 2021 Tuesday that it had removed hundreds of accounts linked to a mysterious advertising agency from Russia that sought to pay social media *influencers to *smear COVID-19 vaccines made by Pfizer and AstraZeneca. A network of 65 Facebook accounts and 243 Instagram accounts was **(83)** traced back to Fazze, an advertising and marketing firm working in Russia **(84)** on behalf of an unknown client.

The network used fake accounts to spread misleading claims that *disparaged the safety of the Pfizer and AstraZeneca vaccines. One claimed AstraZeneca's shot would turn a person into a chimpanzee. The fake accounts targeted India, Latin America and the U.S., using several social media platforms including Facebook and Instagram.

Russia has been actively marketing its COVID-19 vaccine, Sputnik V, abroad in what some analysts see as an effort to score points. But Facebook representatives did not *speculate on the possible reasons behind the smear campaign.

The Fazze network also contacted several countries' social media influencers with offers to pay them for *reposting the misleading content. That *ploy *backfired when influencers in Germany and France exposed the network's scheme.

Along with removing the network's accounts, Facebook also banned Fazze from its platforms.

Fazze's effort did not get much success online, with some posts failing to get even a single response. But, while the campaign may have failed, it's *noteworthy because of its effort to *enlist social media influencers. According to Nathaniel Gleicher, Facebook's head of security policy, **(88)** "Although it was *sloppy and didn't have very good reach, it was an elaborate *setup," he said.

Facebook investigators say some influencers did post the material, but later deleted it when stories about Fazze's work began to emerge.

The offer from Fazze **(89)** urged influencers not to mention that they were being paid, and also suggested they criticize the media's reporting on vaccines. **(90)** "Too many red flags," French YouTouber Léo Grasset told the Associated Press. "I decided not to do it."

注）*influencer 大きな影響を与える人　*smear を中傷する
*disparage の信用を落とす　*speculate 憶測する
*repost 電子掲示板に再度掲載する　*ploy 策略　*backfire 裏目に出る
*noteworthy 注目すべき　*enlist に協力を求める
*sloppy 不注意な、ずさんな　*setup 仕組み

81. What did Facebook do on August 11, 2021?

A. It cancelled all new accounts.
B. It called the police and the President of the United States.
C. It closed hundreds of fake accounts from a mysterious agency.
D. It temporally closed down Facebook for several days.

82. How did the unknown client communicate with the world?

A. Accounts from Facebook and Instagram.
B. Telephones in offices around the world.
C. A massive Tweeting campaign.
D. Mysterious airplanes dropped advertising leaflets around the world.

83. What does the underlined part (83) traced back mean?

A. lost track

B. disagreed with

C. asked about

D. found out

84. What does the underlined part (84) on behalf of mean?

A. the other half

B. success

C. failure

D. representing

85. What did the fake accounts do?

A. They said Facebook was not useful but Twitter was okay.

B. They said Facebook proved Russia made COVID-19 vaccines by Pfizer and AstraZeneca.

C. They claimed Pfizer and AstraZeneca vaccines were dangerous.

D. They said India, Latin America and the U.S. smeared COVID-19 vaccine, Sputnik V.

86. How did the Fazze network spread the smear campaign?

A. Using several social media platforms.

B. Writing to newspapers.

C. Composing music.

D. Creating different vaccines.

87. How did the Fazze network backfire?

A. The influencers advertised the network's offer.

B. The influencers exposed the network's offer.

C. The network refused to pay the influencers.

D. The influencers asked the network to pay more.

88. What does the underlined part (88) "Although it was sloppy and didn't have very good reach, it was an elaborate setup," mean?

A. The setup was stupid from beginning to end.

B. The setup achieved all of its objectives.

C. The setup was brilliant though it failed.

D. The setup made many people famous.

89. **Why did Fazze (89) “urge[d] influencers not to mention that they were being paid, and also suggest[ed] they criticize the media's reporting on vaccines”?**

A. Fazze was kind.

B. Fazze was being tricky.

C. Fazze was confused.

D. Fazze was afraid of Chimpanzees.

90. **What does Grasset mean by the underlined part (90) “Too many red flags,” French YouTuber Léo Grasset told the Associated Press. “I decided not to do it”?**

A. Grasset liked adventure.

B. Grasset liked Fazze.

C. Grasset liked Russia.

D. Grasset sensed something was wrong.

X. 次の会話を読み、設問の答として最も適切なものをA、B、C、Dの中から1つ選びなさい。

Jim : I went shopping for food for us. I was shocked that a group of boys weren't wearing masks.

Minako : What did you do, Jim?

Jim : I got away from them as quickly as I could.

Minako : It's sad. I mean being afraid of people because of COVID-19.

Jim : Yes, very sad. I mostly miss seeing friends, eating out and going to bookstores.

Minako : I agree. At least we two can do all our work from home via our computers.

Jim : And we get along well together all the time.

Minako : Sadly, a lot of families that *sequester together find out they don't like each other. Sometimes that leads to domestic violence.

Jim : And people escape their homes and catch the virus.

Minako : I feel sorry for restaurants that are losing business because of the pandemic.

Jim : I feel sorry for the people who go out to have fun and get sick.

Minako : There are now new *variants of COVID-19. I hope our shots will work against them. I think we'll need a *booster shot.

Jim : If so, I trust our town's progressive mayor will arrange to have the entire town vaccinated.

Minako : It's likely he'll set up a date and time for everyone as he did the first time.

Jim : Tell me honestly. Do you miss eating out and shopping for clothes?

Minako : Well, not that much, really. I do miss our favorite pizza restaurant. I sometimes feel like I'm betraying my friends by not eating there.

Jim : I feel the same way, but we can't take chances.

Minako : True. Speaking of chances, you've lost too much weight, by which I mean muscle.

Jim : I know. You're right.

Minako : We'll walk in the apartment and try other exercises.

注）*sequester を隔離する　*variant 変異株、変異体
*booster shot 効能促進の予防注射、ワクチンなどの追加接種

91. What made Minako sad when Jim returned home from shopping?

A. The staff was rude to Jim.
B. He couldn't find what he wanted.
C. Fearing people who might have COVID-19.
D. Jim was rude to the boys without masks.

92. What do Jim and Minako miss most in the pandemic?

A. They miss seeing friends, and going to bookstores and restaurants.
B. They miss working in an office downtown.
C. They miss traveling.
D. They miss crowded trains.

93. In what ways are Jim and Minako lucky?

A. They can work from home and they like being together.
B. They can take a vacation in Hawaii.
C. They can eat pizza.
D. They can enjoy tennis.

94. What can be the bad side of sequestering?

A. They can escape and avoid COVID-19.
B. Domestic violence.
C. Friendly conversation.
D. Missing the right train.

95. Who do Jim and Minako NOT mention in their conversation?

A. People who get along together at home.
B. Restaurants losing business due to the pandemic.
C. People going out for fun and catching COVID-19.
D. Students studying at school during the pandemic.

96. How do Jim and Minako expect to be taken care of for the "booster" shots for the COVID-19 variants?

A. Very well, judging from the progressive Mayor's previous competence.

B. Very likely it will be pure chaos.

C. It will work only for older people.

D. It will work only for younger people.

97. What does Minako miss very much in the pandemic?

A. Shopping for clothes.

B. Eating at their favorite pizza restaurant.

C. Wearing a mask.

D. Working from home.

98. Why does Minako say, "I sometimes feel like I'm betraying my friends"?

A. She steals money from them.

B. She wants to eat at the pizza restaurant but is afraid to.

C. She does not like pizza anymore.

D. She hopes the pizza restaurant will close.

99. What has Minako noticed is a problem about Jim being sequestered?

A. He has gotten fat and should eat less.

B. His memory is getting weak.

C. He's lost weight and should walk in the apartment and do other exercises.

D. He sleeps too much.

100. What is a good title for this story?

A. Sequestering is Dangerous

B. Jim and Minako Out and About

C. COVID-19 is not a Problem

D. Sequestering is Necessary

マークシート記入例

東京の本会場でC級を受験する、国連 太郎さん、受験番号が「東京01-40001」、生年月日が「1980年10月24日」の場合の記入例です。

【受験番号/氏名】
それぞれ受験票の記載通りに記入してください。

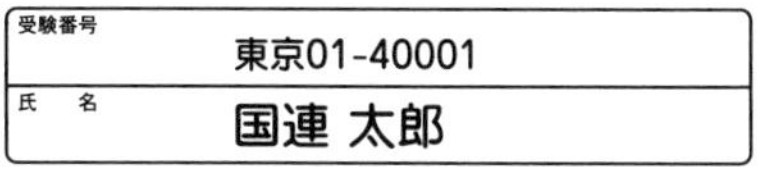

【受験地区】
下段の都道府県部分を塗りつぶしてください。

【会場番号】
都道府県部分に続く2桁の数字を塗りつぶしてください。

【受験番号】
ハイフン（–）以降の5桁の数字を塗りつぶしてください。

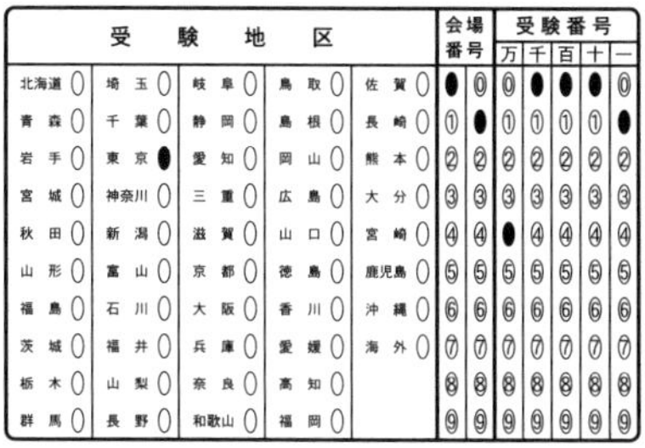

【受験級】
「C」と記入し、下段のC級部分を塗りつぶしてください。

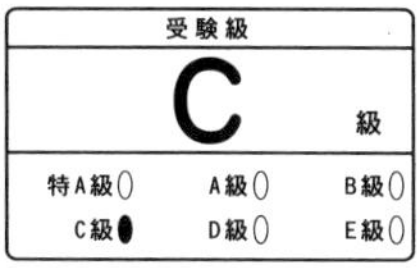

【生年月日】
4桁の西暦・月・日を塗りつぶしてください。
10未満の月・日の十の位は、「0」を塗りつぶしてください。

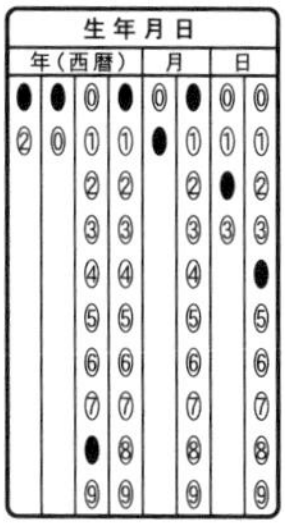

※HB以上の鉛筆を用いてマークをしてください。

※他の地区から会場を変更して受験する場合でも、受験票に記載されている受験地区・会場番号をマークしてください。

2021年
第2回試験
解答・解説

2021年　国連英検C級第2回試験
解答・解説

I　短い英文を2度聴いたあと，
その英文に対して適切な応答を選ぶリスニングテスト。10問出題。

1.　解答：C

解説　話者は相手に長時間の読書で疲れていると伝えているので，選択肢の中で最もふさわしい応答は，Cが正解。

ナレーション　My eyes are tired because I've been reading for a long time.
「長い間読んでいたので目が疲れています」

A. それはいいですね。　B. いつあなたに会えますか。
C. 無理をしないでください。　D. 私はわかりません。

2.　解答：A

解説　話者は相手に洗濯機の使用法を教えてくれるように依頼しているので，選択肢の中で最もふさわしい応答は，Aが正解。

ナレーション　Please explain to me how to use the new washing machine.
「新しい洗濯機の使い方を説明してください」

A. 喜んで。　B. お先にどうぞ。
C. 素晴らしいです。　D. どういたしまして。

3.　解答：D

解説　金物屋さんの場所を尋ねているので，選択肢の中で最もふさわしい応答は，Dが正解。

ナレーション　Do you know where the hardware store is?
「金物屋さんがどこにあるか知っていますか」

A. 私は糊を買いました。　B. お店は鍵を売っています。
C. お店は果物を売っています。　D. それは角にあります。

4.　解答：A

解説 将来なりたいものについて尋ねられているので，選択肢の中で最もふさわしい応答は，A が正解。

ナレーション What would you like to be when you grow up?
「大人になったら何になりたいですか」

A. 外交官。
B. それはここから遠いです。
C. いいえ，私はそれを好きではありません。
D. 私は一生懸命に働かなければなりません。

5.　解答：B

解説 美術館に行ったらどうかと提案しているので，選択肢の中で最もふさわしい応答は，B が正解。

ナレーション How about going to the museum this weekend?
「今週末，美術館に行くのはいかがでしょうか」

A. 私はニュースを聞きました。　B. いいね。
C. それはおいしいです。　D. 私は映画が好きです。

6.　解答：D

解説 歯科医の予約がいつなのか尋ねられているので，選択肢の中で最もふさわしい応答は，D が正解。

ナレーション When is your appointment with your dentist?
「歯医者の予約はいつですか」

A. それは私の家の近くにあります。
B. 私は領収書をもらうのを忘れました。
C. 次の駅です。
D. 次の月曜日です。

7.　解答：A

解説 スーツケースの重量を尋ねられているので，選択肢の中で最もふさわしい応答は，A が正解。

ナレーション How heavy is this suitcase?
「このスーツケースはどのくらいの重さですか」

A. それは 15 キロの重さがあります。　B. それは四角いです。
C. それには名札がついています。　D. それは私のものです。

8.　解答：B

解説　話者は相手に彼の誕生日を祝いたいと述べているので，選択肢の中で最もふさわしい応答は，B が正解。

ナレーション　I'd like to celebrate his birthday.
「私は彼の誕生日を祝いたい」
A. とても寒いです。
B. 驚かせましょう。
C. あなたは切符を持っていますか。
D. 公園に多くの人々がいるのが見えます。

9.　解答：D

解説　コンピューターグラフィックスに興味があるかどうか尋ねられているので，選択肢の中で最もふさわしい応答は，D が正解。

ナレーション　Are you interested in computer graphics?
「コンピューターグラフィックスに興味がありますか」
A. 私は大学へ行きました。　B. 私は先生に会いました。
C. 私は物理が好きではありません。　D. それは面白いです。

10.　解答：B

解説　話者は相手に自分の先生が優しいと伝えているので，選択肢の中で最もふさわしい応答は，B が正解。

ナレーション　My teacher is kind.
「私の先生は優しいです」
A. あなたは遅いです。　B. あなたは幸運です。
C. それは橋の近くです。　D. 私はそれの支払いをしました。

II　短い会話を 2 度聴いたあと，
その内容に関する質問を聴いて答えるリスニングテスト。10 問出題。

11.　解答：B

解説　女性は予防接種をかなり前にしたと言っている。while は「しばらくの間」，quite a while back で「かなり前」の意味。B が正解。

A. 彼は自分のことを気にすべきだ。　B. 彼女はそれをかなり前にした。

C. 彼女はそれを先日した。　D. 彼は家にいるべきだ。

ナレーション

Man:　Have you had your vaccinations yet?

Woman: Quite a while back.

Question　What does the woman mean?

(男)：予防接種はもうお済みですか。

(女)：かなり前に。

質問　女性は何と言っていますか。

12.　解答：A

解説　男性は女性に結婚式に来てもらいたいと言っている。You're invited は「あなたは招待されている」の意味。A が正解。

A. 彼は彼女に結婚式に出席して欲しい。

B. 女性は結婚式に来ないだろう。

C. 男性は彼女に彼と結婚するよう頼んでいる。

D. 女性は彼を結婚式に招待するだろう。

ナレーション

Woman: You are getting married!

Man:　And you're invited to the wedding.

Question　What does the man mean?

(女)：結婚するんですね。

(男)：それであなたを結婚式に招待する予定です。

質問　男性は何と言っていますか。

13.　解答：D

解説　女性は外食したいと言っている。D が正解。

A. 彼は 1 人でレストランに行くでしょう。

B. 彼女は夕食を作るでしょう。

C. 彼女は友達を夕食に招くでしょう。

D. 彼らは一緒にレストランに行くでしょう。

ナレーション

Man:　　I'll be back early.

Woman: Let's eat out then!

Question　What does the woman mean?

(男)：早く帰ってくるよ。

(女)：じゃあ，外食しましょう。

質問　女性は何と言っていますか。

14.　解答：C

解説　男性は映画を見に行こうと言っている。C が正解。

A. 彼は休暇を取らないだろう。

B. 彼は仕事の後，彼女を家に連れて帰るだろう。

C. 彼は彼女と一緒に映画を見るだろう。

D. 彼はとても忙しい。

ナレーション

Woman: I want a day off!

Man:　　Let's go see a movie.

Question　What does the man mean?

(女)：休みが欲しいわ。

(男)：映画を見に行こう。

質問　男性は何と言っていますか。

15.　解答：B

解説　女性は立派な屋根職人を知っていると言っている。B が正解。

A. 彼女の家は新しい屋根が必要だ。

B. 彼女は腕のいい屋根職人を知っている。

C. 彼はすでに屋根職人を雇っている。

D. 彼女は屋根職人が彼女に必要だと思っている。

ナレーション

Man:　　My house needs a new roof.

Woman: I know a really great roofer.

Question　What does the woman mean?

(男)：僕の家は新しい屋根が必要なんだ。

(女)：私はすごく素晴らしい屋根職人を知っています。

質問　女性は何と言っていますか。

16.　解答：A

解説　男性は女性の言っていることが面白そうだと言っている。A が正解。

A. 彼は彼女の考えが気に入っているようだ。

B. 彼は飛行機の操縦方法を学んでいるところだ。

C. 彼は自分の飛行機を操縦するのが楽しい。

D. 彼は女性の気が変だと思っている。

ナレーション

Woman: I'm learning how to fly.

Man: That's really interesting.

Question　What does the man mean?

(女)：飛行機の操縦方法を学んでいるところです。

(男)：それは本当に興味深いですね。

質問　男性は何と言っていますか。

17.　解答：A

解説　女性はプロポーズされた驚きとうれしい気持ちを "Wow!" と言って表現し，次にもっと早くプロポーズして欲しかったと言っている。A が正解。

A. 彼女はワクワクしている。

B. 彼女は彼が結婚していたのを知らなかった。

C. 彼女は興味がない。

D. 彼女はすでに結婚している。

ナレーション

Man: Would you like to marry me?

Woman: Wow! What took you so long?

Question　What does the woman mean?

(男)：僕と結婚してくれませんか。

(女)：うわー！　どうしてそんなに時間がかかったの？

質問　女性は何と言っていますか。

18.　解答：B

解説　男性は 2，3 冊本を読むと言っている。男性は a couple とだけ言っているが，文脈からa couple of booksという意味。a couple ofは「2, 3の」の意味。Bが正解。

A. 彼はたくさん本を読む。　B. 彼は2，3冊本を読む。

C. 彼は全然本を読まない。　D. 彼はカップルについての本を読む。

ナレーション

Woman: How many books do you read a month?

Man: Oh, I usually read a couple.

Question　What does the man mean?

(女)：月に何冊くらい本を読みますか。

(男)：えーっと，たいてい2，3冊読みます。

質問　男性は何と言っていますか。

19.　解答：B

解説　女性はマスクがなくなったと言う男性の安全を心配して，もちろんと言っている。Bが正解。

A. 彼女はお金が稼げるのでうれしい。

B. 彼女は彼の安全をとても心配している。

C. 彼女は彼がマスクをくれるのでうれしい。

D. 彼女はどうしていいのかわからない。

ナレーション

Man: Could you give me a mask? I've run out.

Woman: Why, of course!

Question　What does the woman mean?

(男)：マスクをいただけますか。もうなくなったので。

(女)：もちろんだわ。

質問　女性は何と言っていますか。

20.　解答：C

解説　男性は医者に行っていたと言っている。Cが正解。

A. 彼は美術展に行っていた。　B. 彼はずっと家にいる。

C. 彼は医者に診てもらっていた。　D. 彼はニューヨークに行っていた。

ナレーション

Woman: Where have you been all day?

Man:　At the doctor's. Don't worry. I'm fine.
Question　What does the man mean?
(女)：あなたはきょう1日，どこにいたの？
(男)：お医者さんに行っていたんだ。心配しないで。大丈夫だよ。
質問　男性は何と言っていますか。

III　まとまりのある内容の英文（300語前後）を2度聴いたあと，その内容に関する英語の質問を聴いて答えるリスニングテスト。10問出題。

21.　解答：B

解説　"This is the story of my hearing aid." とジョージが話を始め，結果として気に入った補聴器を買うことができたことから，正解はB。
A. 買い物　B. ジョージに補聴器を買うこと
C. ユーコに補聴器を買うこと　D. ジョージの耳元で叫ぶこと

22.　解答：D

解説　ジョージの年齢に関する言及はないので，正解はD。
A. 70歳ぐらい　B. 60歳ぐらい
C. 50歳ぐらい　D. 年齢は述べられていない

23.　解答：A

解説　"Get in the car. We're going shopping for a hearing aid." とユーコが言っていることから，正解はA。
A. 彼らは自動車で行った。　B. 彼らは歩いた。
C. 彼らは列車に乗った。　D. 彼らはバスを使った。

24.　解答：A

解説　"Before shopping, we drove to our ear doctor." から，正解はA。
A. 耳鼻科に行った
B. デパートに行った
C. 高価で使い心地の悪い補聴器を買った
D. お気に入りの大型量販店に行った

25. 解答：D

解説 "He was a kind old man who gave me a series of tests and concluded that while my hearing was not bad, I would be happier with a hearing aid. He explained the various hearing aids and said the best were rechargeable and the second best used small batteries." から，正解は D。

A. 彼はジョージにいろいろな検査をした。

B. 彼はさまざまな種類の補聴器の説明をした。

C. 彼は充電式の補聴器がいちばんいいと言った。

D. 彼はジョージに電池式の補聴器を売った。

26. 解答：B

解説 "We went to two department stores and discovered their hearing aids were uncomfortable and too expensive." から，正解は B。

A. デパートでは補聴器を売っていなかった。

B. 彼はデパートの補聴器は高価で，使い心地が悪かった。

C. デパートの補聴器は快適だった。

D. デパートの補聴器は安かった。

27. 解答：D

解説 "I was given a series of hearing tests. I liked the rechargeable hearing aid best, even though it was expensive." "The hearing aid center here will adjust your hearing aid for free." から，正解は D。

A. ジョージは一連の聴力検査を受けた。

B. 彼は高価だが充電式の補聴器が気に入った。

C. ジョージは補聴器を無料で調整してもらえることを知った。

D. 上記はすべて正しい。

28. 解答：A

解説 "Is it comfortable?" she asked. "That's what is most important." とユーコがジョージに言っていることから，正解は A。

A. 補聴器の使い心地がいいこと　　B. 補聴器が安いこと

C. 補聴器が魅力的であること　　D. B と C の両方が正しい

29. 解答：A

解説 "I'm especially happy you can hear me once again," とユーコが言っていることから，正解は A。

A. ジョージは再び彼女の声を聞くことができた。

B. 彼女は買い物に行くことができた。

C. 彼女はお金を節約することができた。

D. 彼女は耳鼻科に行くことができた。

30. 解答：C

解説 会話の最後で "I'm glad we did this," I said. とジョージが言い，"I'm especially happy you can hear me once again," Yuko said. ユーコが言っていることから，正解は C。

A. 買い物に行こう

B. 耳鼻科医の世界

C. いかに補聴器がジョージとユーコを幸せにしたのか

D. 補聴器ができるまで

ナレーション

This is the story of my hearing aid. It began like this.

"You need a hearing aid, George," my wife, Yuko, said.

"What did you say?" I said.

"I'm tired of shouting in your ear, George. We are going to get you a hearing aid today. Did you hear what I said?"

"What?"

"Get in the car. We're going shopping for a hearing aid."

Before shopping, we drove to our ear doctor. He was a kind old man who gave me a series of tests and concluded that while my hearing was not bad, I would be happier with a hearing aid. He explained the various hearing aids and said the best were rechargeable and the second best used small batteries.

We went to two department stores and discovered their hearing aids were uncomfortable and too expensive.

"Let's drive to our favorite American wholesale store," Yuko said.

"They sell hearing aids. And I trust them."

We went to the hearing aid division of the store. I was given a series of hearing tests. I liked the rechargeable hearing aid best, even though it was expensive.

"Is this hearing aid too expensive?" I asked Yuko.

"Is it comfortable?" she asked. "That's what is most important."

"It's excellent," I said.

"The hearing aid center here will adjust your hearing aid for free."

"I'm glad we did this," I said.

"I'm especially happy you can hear me once again," Yuko said.

Questions 21. What is most important in this story?

22. How old is George?

23. How did George and Yuko go shopping for a hearing aid?

24. What did George and Yuko do first?

25. What is one thing the ear doctor did NOT do?

26. What did George and Yuko find out when they went to the two department stores?

27. What happened at their favorite American wholesale store?

28. What was most important about the hearing aids to Yuko?

29. What made Yuko especially happy?

30. What is the best title for this story?

訳例　これは，私の補聴器の話です。はじまりはこんな感じでした。

「補聴器が必要ね，ジョージ」妻のユーコが言いました。

「何て言ったの？」と私は言いました。

「耳元で大声を出すのはうんざりだわ，ジョージ。きょう，補聴器を買いましょう。私が言ったことが聞こえたの？」

「何て言ったの？」

「車に乗ってね。補聴器を買いに行きましょう。」

買い物の前に，車で耳鼻科に行きました。ドクターは親切なおじいさんで，いろいろな検査をしてくれて，聴力はそんなに悪くないが，補聴器をつけたほうがいいだろうという結論になりました。補聴器にはいろいろな種類があり，充電式が一番で，小型電池を使うものが二番だと説明してくれました。
私たちは２つのデパートに行きましたが，その店の補聴器は使い心地が悪く，値段も高すぎることがわかりました。
「私たちのお気に入りのアメリカの大型量販店に行ってみましょう」とユーコが言いました。「あそこなら補聴器も売っているし，信用できるわ。」
私たちは，その店の補聴器売り場に行きました。私はいろいろな聴力検査を受けました。私は高かったけれど充電式の補聴器がいちばん気に入りました。
「この補聴器は高すぎるかな？」と私はユーコに尋ねました。
「使い心地はいいかしら？」と彼女は尋ねました。「それがいちばん大事なことだわ。」
「素晴らしいよ」と私は言いました。
「ここの補聴器センターは無料で調整してくれるのよ」
「買ってよかったね」と私は言いました。
「再び私の声が聞こえるようになって本当にうれしいわ」とユーコは言いました。

質問　21. この物語で最も重要なことは何ですか。
22. ジョージは何歳ですか。
23. ジョージとユーコはどのように補聴器を買いに行ったのですか。
24. ジョージとユーコは最初に何をしましたか。
25. 耳鼻科医がしなかったことは何ですか。
26. ジョージとユーコは２つのデパートに行って，何がわかりましたか。
27. ２人の好きなアメリカの大型量販店で何が起こりましたか。
28. ユーコにとって補聴器の何がいちばん重要だったのでしょうか。
29. ユーコが特にうれしかったことは何ですか。
30. この話の題名に最もふさわしいものは何ですか。

IV

会話を２度聴いたあと，
その内容に関する英語の質問を聴いて答えるリスニングテスト。10問出題。

31.　解答：C

解説　リカが “It means to swim.” と言っていることから，正解はC。
A. リカが授業を始めることを意味する。
B. リカが授業で役に立つ表現について話すだろう。

C. 泳ぐことを意味する。
D. リカは家に帰るだろう。

32.　解答：B

解説 ジローが "Do you know "surf's up"? It's a useful expression." と言っていることから，正解は B。

A. 彼はビーチに向かっている。
B. 彼は先生に英語で「役に立つ表現」を知っていることを見せたい。
C. 彼は満潮が来るのを心配している。
D. 彼は危険を感じている。

33.　解答：A

解説 リカが"Yes, but I've never thought of it as simply a "useful expression." To me it means getting into my wetsuit and heading straight for the beach." と言っていることから，正解は A。

A. 彼女はそれが本当にサーフィンをすることを意味しているとジローに伝えたい。
B. 彼女は海を恐れている。
C. 彼女はジローの表情が堅苦しいと思っている。
D. 彼女は "surf's up" の意味を理解していない。

34.　解答：C

解説 リカがジローに "I understand you are studying Mark Twain for your graduation thesis." と言っていることから，正解は C。

A. 三島由紀夫　B. アーネスト・ヘミングウェイ
C. マーク・トウェイン　D. エミリー・ディキンソン

35.　解答：A

解説 ジローが "It's hard to pronounce in English." と言っていることから，正解は A。

A. 彼は "Huckleberry" を発音することができない。
B. 彼は "Finn" が本の正しい題名だと信じている。
C. 彼は "Finn" の方がより丁寧だと考えている。

D. 彼は姓が名の前に来るべきだと思っている。

36.　解答：C

解説　リカが“Don't you know anything except a few English expressions?” と言っていることから，正解は C。

A. あなたはなぜ英語がそんなに上手なのですか。

B. あなたの英語は少し硬いですが，悪くはないです。

C. あなたは英語の表現を少ししか知らないようですね。

D. あなたはほとんど英語のネイティブスピーカーのようです。

37.　解答：B

解説　ジローが “I'm also reading Finn in Japanese.” と言っていることから，正解は B。

A. 英語のみで　　B. 日本語で

C. 英語と日本語で同等に　　D. 英語とドイツ語で

38.　解答：D

解説　ジローが “Back in Japan, all we had were useful expressions in English, plus grammar translation. We also had easy English conversations in English class.” と言っていることから，正解は D。

A. 英米文学に対する批判的思考

B. 自分の気持ちを英語で書くこと

C. 英語でのエッセイに関する会話

D. 役に立つ表現，文法と訳，簡単な会話

39.　解答：C

解説　リカが “We'll be studying short stories and poems in English and writing about them in English.” と言っていることから，正解は C。

A. 彼女は簡単な英会話の録音を流すだろう。

B. 彼女は全て日本語で講義をするだろう。

C. 彼女は短編小説や詩を教え，受講生にそれについて英語で書かせるだろう。

D. 彼女は簡単な会話を英語で教えるだろう。

40. 解答：D

解説 リカが“It will be like the California surf. Sometimes it will be easy on you and sometimes it will knock you off your board and send you flying. I'll be like your lifeguard, never letting you drown.”と英語学習をサーフィンを学ぶことに，リカをライフガードに例え，よりわかりやすく説明していることから，正解はD。

A. 彼女はサーフィンとライフガードが好きだ。

B. 彼女はライフガードの仕事が好きではない。

C. 英語学習者の仕事は，ライフガードの仕事に似ている。

D. ジローにとって英語学習やリカのことをより理解できる。

ナレーション

Rika teaches English and American Literature at a university in California. Jiro is her summer English student from Japan.

Jiro: Hello, how are you?

Rika: I'm fine. The weather is great for surfing. Are you going in after class?

Jiro: What do you mean by “going in”?

Rika: It means to swim. Do you like to swim?

Jiro: Oh yes! Surf's up. Do you know “surf's up”? It's a useful expression.

Rika: Yes, but I've never thought of it as simply a “useful expression.” To me it means getting into my wetsuit and heading straight for the beach. I understand you are studying Mark Twain for your graduation thesis. That's great. What are you writing about?

Jiro: Finn.

Rika: What Finn? You mean Huckleberry Finn?

Jiro: Yes. It's hard to pronounce in English. I'm writing my thesis in Japanese. I'm also reading Finn in Japanese.

Rika: Huckleberry Finn! Don't you know anything except a few English expressions?

Jiro: Back in Japan, all we had were useful expressions in English, plus grammar translation. We also had easy English conversations in

English class. I'd like to speak natural English like you, sensei.

Rika: You are in luck. We'll be studying short stories and poems in English and writing about them in English. And when you feel the power of the California surf under your surfboard you will know the full meaning of "surf's up."

Jiro: Will it be hard?

Rika: It will be like the California surf. Sometimes it will be easy on you and sometimes it will knock you off your board and send you flying. I'll be like your lifeguard, never letting you drown.

Jiro: I'm looking forward to the challenge!

Questions 31. What does Rika mean by "going in?"

32. Why does Jiro use the expression "surf's up"?

33. Why does Rika say that "surf's up" is not "simply a useful expression" to her?

34. Which writer is Jiro studying?

35. Why does Jiro call the novel he is studying "Finn"?

36. After discussing Huckleberry Finn what does Rika say to Jiro?

37. In what language is Jiro reading Huckleberry Finn?

38. What did Jiro learn in English class back in Japan?

39. How will Rika help Jiro speak natural English in their class?

40. Why does Rika compare English learning to surfing and herself to a lifeguard?

訳例　リカはカリフォルニアの大学で英米文学を教えています。ジローは日本から来た彼女の夏期英語を学ぶ留学生です。

ジロー：こんにちは，お元気ですか？

リカ：　元気よ。サーフィンをするには最高の天気ね。授業が終わったら行くの？

ジロー："going in" ってどういう意味ですか。

リカ：　泳ぐという意味よ。泳ぐのは好き？

ジロー：ええ，もちろん。Surf's up. "surf's up" って知っていますか。便利な表現ですよね。

リカ：　そうね，でもそれを単に「便利な表現」だと思ったことはないわ。私にとっては，ウェットスーツを着て，ビーチにまっすぐ向かうという意味だわ。あなたは卒業論文でマーク・トウェインの研究しているのね。素晴らしいことだわ。どんなことを書いているの？

ジロー：フィン。

リカ：「フィン」って？ 『ハックルベリー・フィン』のこと？

ジロー：そうです。英語では発音しにくいんです。僕は日本語で卒論を書いています。『フィン』も日本語で読んでいるんですよ。

リカ：『ハックルベリー・フィン』！ ほんの少ししか英語の表現を知らないの？

ジロー：日本では，英語の便利な表現と文法と訳読しか勉強しなかったのです。英語の授業では簡単な英会話もありました。先生みたいに自然な英語を話してみたいです。

リカ：あなたは運がいいわ。短編小説や詩を英語で勉強して，それについて英語で書いてもらうわ。そして，カリフォルニアの波のパワーをサーフボードの下で感じたら，“surf’s up” の本当の意味がわかるようになるでしょう。

ジロー：難しいですか。

リカ：カリフォルニアの波と同じよ。時には優しく，時にはボードから叩き落とされ，飛ばされるでしょう。私はあなたのライフガードのように，あなたを決して溺れさせないようにするわ。

ジロー：チャレンジを楽しみにしています。

質問 31. リカの言う “going in” の意味は何ですか。

32. ジローはなぜ “surf’s up” という表現を使うのですか。

33. リカはなぜ “surf’s up” を「単に便利な表現」ではないと言うのですか。

34. ジローはどの作家を研究していますか。

35. ジローは研究している小説をなぜ『フィン』と呼ぶのですか。

36. 『ハックルベリー・フィン』について話し合った後，リカはジローに何と言いますか。

37. ジローは何語で『ハックルベリー・フィン』を読んでいますか。

38. ジローは日本の英語の授業で何を学びましたか。

39. リカはジローが自然な英語を話すように授業でどのように支援するのですか。

40. リカはなぜ，英語の勉強をサーフィンに，そして自分をライフガードに例えるのですか。

V 英文の下線部の意味を最もよく表す語または語句を4つの選択肢中から1つ選ぶ問題。10問出題。

41. 解答：C

解説 go broke は「文なしになる」の意味なので，C が正解。

訳例 彼はラスベガスで一文なしになりました。

A. 盗まれた　B. 道に迷った　C. 貧しくなった　D. 滞在していた

42. 解答：B

解説 too careless は「不注意すぎる」の意味なので，B が正解。

訳例 彼は運転が不注意すぎます。

A. 非常に注意深い　B. 危険な
C. とても楽しい　D. 場所を見つけるのがうまい

43. 解答：C

解説 highly estimated は「高く評価されている」の意味なので，C が正解。

訳例 私たちの市長は，非常に高く評価されています。

A. 非常に裕福な　B. 抜け目のない
C. とても尊敬されている　D. 背が高い

44. 解答：D

解説 down は「落ち込んだ，元気がない」の意味なので，D が正解。

訳例 彼は落ち込んでいます。

A. お金持ちの　B. 非常に幸せな
C. 何かを見つけるところの　D. 不幸な

45. 解答：C

解説 great pool player は「立派なビリヤードのプレーヤー」の意味なので，C が正解。

訳例 彼女はビリヤードの名手です。

A. 水泳プールの掃除係　B. 相乗り自動車の主催者
C. 賢明なビリヤードのプレーヤー　D. 速い水泳の選手

46. 解答：A

解説 keyed-up は形容詞で「緊張した」の意味なので，A が正解。

訳例　彼は会議の前に緊張していました。
A. 緊張して　B. 冷静な
C. 要領の悪い　D. ユーモアのある

47. 解答：B

解説　belong to は「に所属する」の意味なので，B が正解。

訳例　彼女は学会に所属しています。
A. 所有する　B. の一員だ　C. 嫌う　D. もう所属していない

48. 解答：A

解説　advance は「前払金」の意味なので，A が正解。

訳例　彼女の出版社は彼女に本の前金を支払いました。
A. お金　B. 賛美　C. 情報　D. アドバイス

49. 解答：D

解説　cope with は「うまく処理する」の意味なので，D が正解。

訳例　私はまだ問題に対処しています。
A. 楽しんでいる　B. 忘れようとしている
C. 感心している　D. 対処している

50. 解答：D

解説　be open to は「受け入れる用意がある，余地のある」の意味なので，D が正解。

訳例　彼はみんなの意見に耳を傾けてくれます。
A. について気にしない　B. 理解しない
C. に無関心だ　D. を気にかける

VI　300 ～ 400 語程度のまとまりのある文を国連英検指定テキスト『新 わかりやすい国連の活動と世界』から抜粋し，その内容を把握しているかどうかを問う問題。10 題出題。

51. 解答：C

解説　“the Commission on Human Rights had been the core United Nations body responsible for the promotion and protection of human rights.” から，C が正解。

訳例　人権委員会の主な仕事は何ですか。

A. 総会の広報　B. ボランティア活動の促進
C. 人権の促進と保護　D. 2005 年世界サミット開催に関するアドバイス

52. 解答：A

解説 “Whereas the Commission had made many achievements in this field through its sixty-year history, its politicization had faced severe criticism.” から，A が正解。

訳例 なぜ人権委員会は，成果を出しているにもかかわらず批判されたのですか。
A. 人権委員会に政治的偏向があった。
B. 人権委員会は任務をよく遂行した。
C. 人権委員会は国連のために働くのを止めた。
D. 人権委員会は数人の政治家を委員会に招待した。

53. 解答：B

解説 “The 2005 World Summit, in its Outcome, endorsed the creation of the Human Rights Council” から，B が正解。

訳例 誰が人権理事会の創設を支持しましたか。
A. 2006 年の総会　B. 2005 年の世界サミット
C. 特別な代表者　D. 特別な報告者

54. 解答：C

解説 “The Sub-Commission on the Promotion and Protection of Human Rights was likewise superseded by the Human Rights Council Advisory Committee.” から，C が正解。

訳例 何が人権促進保護小委員会にとって代わりましたか。
A. 人権委員会　B. 総会　C. 人権理事会諮問委員会　D. 国連加盟国

55. 解答：B

解説 “The Human Rights Council comprises 47 Member States” から，B が正解。

訳例 人権理事会にはいくつの加盟国がありますか。
A. 42 カ国　B. 47 カ国　C. 51 カ国　D. 60 カ国

56. 解答：D

解説 “The Council members shall pledge to contribute to the promoting and protecting of human rights.” から，D が正解。

訳例 理事会の加盟国は何をするのですか。

A. 加盟国を選出する。 B. 国連憲章を作る。 C. 地理の専門家になる。
D. 人権の促進と保護に関する貢献について誓約する。

57. 解答：A

解説 “The Universal Periodic Review (UPR) mechanism, newly launched by the Human Rights Council, monitors and examines human rights situations in all United Nations Member States.” から，A が正解。

訳例 国連加盟国において誰が人権状況をモニターし審査するのですか。

A. 普遍的定期審査の機構 B. 国連憲章
C. 世界人権宣言 D. 国際人道法

58. 解答：C

解説 “The Complaint Procedure, formerly known as the 1503 procedure, has also been established by the Council to address consistent patters of gross and reliably attested violations of all human rights and all fundamental freedoms” から，C が正解。

訳例 不服審査手続きはどんなことに対処しますか。

A. 議席の公平な配分 B. 加盟国による自発的な誓約
C. 人権とすべての基本的自由についての侵害 D. 国連の利益促進と保護

59. 解答：C

解説 victim は「被害者」の意味だから，C が正解。

訳例 下線部 (59) victims の意味は何ですか。

A. 違反者 B. 研究者 C. 苦しんでいる人 D. 雇用人

60. 解答：B

解説 address は他動詞で「対処する」の意味だから，B が正解。

訳例 下線部 (60) address の意味は何ですか。

A. 選ぶ B. 対処する C. 確認する D. 形成する

訳例　1946年より，人権委員会は，人権の促進と保護に責任をもつ国連の中心機関として責任を果たしてきた。この分野における人権委員会の60年の歴史と成果の一方で，人権委員会の政治化について強い批判が向けられた。2005年の世界サミットでは，その成果文書の中で，国連人権機構の一層の強化のために，人権理事会の創設を支持した。2006年3月15日に決議60/251を採択することにより総会が創設した人権理事会が，人権委員会に代わることになった。人権促進保護小委員会は人権理事会諮問委員会が代わることになった。

人権理事会は総会で選出された47の加盟国代表から構成され，その構成は地理的に公平な配分に基づく。理事国は，人権の促進と保護に関する貢献について誓約する。選出された理事国は，人権の促進と保護において最高度の水準を保持するものとする。

人権理事会が新しく発足させた普遍的定期審査（Universal Periodic Review: UPR）では，国連加盟国の人権状況のモニターと審査が行われる。1年に42カ国の人権状況が，国連憲章，世界人権宣言，当該国が批准した条約，国家による自発的な誓約および国際人道法に基づいて審査される。人権理事会諮問委員会は，18名の専門家から成り，人権理事会の「シンクタンク」として機能し，人権問題の諸テーマについて理事会に助言する機能を負っている。不服審査手続は，1503手続きとして知られていたものを引き継いで人権理事会により設けられ，世界のあらゆる場所，状況下で起きたすべての人権とすべての基本的自由についての侵害で重大かつ信頼できる証拠のある一貫した形態を示すものに対処する。状況は，人権侵害の被害者により提出された通報と当事国との非公式な協議に基づいて，非公開で審査される。人権理事会は，また，特別手続も扱っている。理事会は，特別報告者，特別代表および作業部会を職務権限保有者として任命し，それらの職務権限保有者は，テーマ別もしくは国別の観点から特定の人権状況に対処し，その状況について公開で報告をし助言を行う。

『新 わかりやすい国連の活動と世界』pp. 58–59

Ⅶ　2つの文章に共通して用いられる語を1つ，選択肢の中から選ぶ問題。
10問出題。

61.　解答：C

解説　backは副詞で「戻って，帰って」，get off O's backで「（人）を悩ますのをやめる」の意味。正解はC。

訳例　「私はすぐに戻ります」
「ほっといてくれ」
A. 頭　　B. 前方　　D. 足

62. 解答：B

解説 can は助動詞で Can you ...? で「…してくれませんか」，名詞で「容器」，garbage can で「ごみ入れ」の意味。正解は B。

訳例 「助けていただけますか」
「ゴミ箱に入れてください」
A. ドア　C. するつもりである　D. 沈む

63. 解答：A

解説 shot は名詞で「注射，写真」の意味。正解は A。

訳例 「あなたは注射を打ってもらう必要があります」
「新しいカメラで素敵な写真が撮れました」
B. 飲み物　C. 自動車　D. ドア

64. 解答：C

解説 fence は名詞で「柵，垣」，自動詞で「フェンシングをする」の意味。正解は C。

訳例 「その猫は柵を乗り越えた」
「あなたにフェンシングの仕方を教えましょう」
A. 屋根　B. 壁　D. 棚

65. 解答：B

解説 blue は形容詞で「元気のない，青い」の意味。正解は B。

訳例 「きょう，私は元気がありません」
「私は青い自転車が欲しい」
A. 黄　C. 紫　D. 銀

66. 解答：A

解説 green は形容詞で「(嫉妬深さを表し) 青ざめた，緑の」，の意味。正解は A。

訳例 「彼は嫉妬に駆られています」
「葉っぱがまた緑色になりました」
B. 灰色　C. 狂気の　D. オレンジ色

67.　解答：D

解説　fair は形容詞で「天気のよい，公正な」の意味。正解は D。

訳例　「船は快晴の中，出航した」
「選挙は公正ではなかった」
A. 雨の　B. 曇った　C. 熱帯の

68.　解答：C

解説　everybody は名詞で「みんな，だれでも」，not everyone で「だれもが…というわけではない」の意味。正解は C。

訳例　「そのフェスティバルは，だれでも楽しめる内容になっていました」
「だれもが有名になる必要があるわけではありません」
A. 販売　B. 自由な　D. 岩

69.　解答：D

解説　schedule は名詞で「予定」，on schedule で「予定通り，定刻通り」他動詞で「予定を立てる」の意味。正解は D。

訳例　「飛行機は予定通り運行しました」
「あなたは予定を立てなければなりません」
A. 水　B. 時間　C. ガソリン

70.　解答：C

解説　news は名詞で「ニュース，新情報」の意味。正解は C。

訳例　「そのウェブサイトはニュースが充実しています」
「あら，それは初耳です」
A. スポーツ　B. ゲーム　D. おしゃべり

VIII　4つの文章の中で，文法的に用法が間違っているものを見つける問題。
10問出題。

71.　解答：D

in the front → in front

「前方の自動車が速度を上げた」

解説　front の用法を問う問題。A の front は「前線」，B の in front of は「の正面に」，C の at the front of (the classroom) は「(教室の) 最前列に」の意味。D は in front で「前方に」の意味なので，in the front ではな

く in front が正しい。D が正解。

訳例　A. シベリアから寒冷前線が下りてきている。
　　　B. 私の目の前に高いビルがある。
　　　C. 彼はいつも教室のいちばん前に座る。

72.　解答：B

from → at

「そのデパートは 10 時に開店する」

解説　from の用法を問う問題。A の (graduate) from は「(学校) を卒業する」，C の from は「(位置の起点) …から」，D の from は「(原因) …で」die from starvation「餓死する」の意味。B は (open) at で「…時から (店が開店する)」の意味なので，from ではなく at が正しい。B が正解。

訳例　A. 私は東京の大学を卒業した。
　　　C. 彼らはニューヨークからパリに引っ越した。
　　　D. 多くの人々が餓死した。

73.　解答：C

at the job → on the job

「その夫婦は仕事を通して会った」

解説　job の用法を問う問題。A の do a great job は「素晴らしい仕事をする，立派にやってのける」，B の a full-time job は「常勤の仕事」，D の a dead-end job は「将来性のない仕事」の意味。C は on the job で「仕事を通して，仕事で」の意味なので，at the job ではなく on the job が正しい。C が正解。

訳例　A. 彼女は素晴らしい仕事をした。
　　　B. 彼は正社員になることを希望している。
　　　D. 誰も将来性のない仕事はしたくない。

74.　解答：A

go on a strike → go on strike

「従業員はストライキをするだろう」

解説　strike の用法を問う問題。B の struck は strike の過去形で「(マッチ) をする」strike a match で「マッチをつける」，C の will strike は「(災害などが) 襲うだろう」，D の struck は strike の過去形で「ぶつける」の意味。A の go on strike は「ストライキに入る」の意味なので，go on a strike ではなく go on strike が正しい。A が正解。

訳例　B. その少女は最後のマッチをつけた。
C. 台風がその地方を襲うだろう。
D. 彼はドアに足をぶつけた。

75.　解答：B

short of → short for

「トムはトマスを短くした呼び名である」

解説 short の用法を問う問題。A の in short は「手短に言うと，要するに」，C の short cut は「近道」，D の stop short は「突然止まる」の意味。B は short for で「…を省略した」の意味なので，short of ではなく short for が正しい。B が正解。

訳例　A. 要するに，彼の人生は幸せだった。
C. 博物館への近道を教えてくれませんか。
D. 列車が突然止まった。

76.　解答：A

all student → all the students

「私はクラスの生徒全員が好きです」

解説 all の用法を問う問題。B の all but は「…の他は皆」，C の all over the place は「至る所で，あちこちで」，D の of all days は「よりによって，こともあろうに」の意味。A の all the students は「生徒全員」の意味なので，all student ではなく all the students が正しい。A が正解。

訳例　B. 1 人の生徒を除いて全員が家に帰った。
C. その母親は至る所で自分の子供を探した。
D. よりによって，彼は自分の誕生日に頭痛がした。

77.　解答：C

roots vegetable → root vegetable

「私は根菜が好きです」

解説 root の用法を問う問題。A の the root of the problem は「その問題の根本」，B の by the roots は「根こそぎに」，D の root out は「を根絶する」の意味。C は root vegetable で「根菜」の意味なので，roots vegetable

ではなく root vegetable が正しい。C が正解。

訳例　A. 彼らは問題の根本を議論した。
B. リスは植物を根こそぎ掘り起こした。
D. 私たちはいじめを根絶しなければならない。

78.　解答：B

small income → a small income

「彼の収入は少ない」

解説　small の用法を問う問題。A の feel small は「肩身の狭い思いをする，気がひける」，C の in a small voice は「小声で」，D の till the small hours は「明け方近くまで」の意味。B は a small income で「わずかな収入」の意味なので，small income ではなく a small income が正しい。B が正解。

訳例　A. 有名人の中で彼女は肩身の狭い思いをした。
C. 彼女は小声で答えた。
D. 彼は明け方近くまで本を読むのが好きだ。

79.　解答：D

features of → features

「その映画は俳優が有名な作曲家を演じています」

解説　feature の用法を問う問題。A の features は「特集する」，B の features は「特徴，機能」，C の feature は「の特徴がある」の意味。D は他動詞の feature で「(俳優など) を (…の役で) 主演させる」の意味なので，features of ではなく features が正しい。D が正解。

訳例　A. 雑誌にその科学者の記事が特集されている。
B. 新しいコンピューターには特別な機能がある。
C. そのレストランはシーフード料理が特徴です。

80.　解答：D

on the purpose → on purpose

「彼は故意に間違ったのではなかった」

解説　purpose の用法を問う問題。A の for practical purposes は「実際上は，実質的には，便宜上」，B の purpose は「目的」，C の a sense of purpose は「生きがい，目的意識」の意味。D は on purpose で「故意に，わざ

と」の意味なので，on the purpose ではなく on purpose が正しい。D が正解。

訳例 A. 彼は論文の中で，便宜上いくつかの写真を使った。
B. 彼女がウィーンに行く目的は音楽を勉強するためだ。
C. 彼女は生きがいを持っている。

IX

300 語前後のまとまりのある文を読み，読解力を試す問題。
空所補充，語句の並べ替え，語彙力，行間を読む力を問う問題を 10 問出題。

81. 解答：C

解説 "Facebook reported on August 11, 2021 Tuesday that it had removed hundreds of accounts" から，C が正解。

訳例 2021 年 8 月 11 日にフェイスブックは何をしましたか。
A. すべての新規アカウントを取り消した。
B. 警察とアメリカ大統領に連絡した。
C. 謎の代理店の数百の偽アカウントを閉鎖した。
D. 数日間フェイスブックを一時的に閉鎖した。

82. 解答：A

解説 "A network of 65 Facebook accounts and 243 Instagram accounts was traced back to Fazze" から，A が正解。

訳例 無名のクライアントは，どのように世界とコミュニケーションをとりましたか。
A. フェイスブックやインスタグラムのアカウント
B. 世界中のオフィスの電話
C. 大規模なツイートキャンペーン
D. 謎の飛行機が世界中に広告ビラを投下した。

83. 解答：D

解説 trace back は「突き止める，捜し出す」の意味だから，D が正解。

訳例 下線部 (83) traced back の意味は何ですか。
A. 見失った　B. 反対した　C. 問い合わせた　D. 発見した

84. 解答：D

解説 on behalf of は「を代表して」の意味だから，D が正解。

訳例 下線部 (84) on behalf of の意味は何ですか。

A. 残りの半分　B. 成功　C. 失敗　D. 代表して

85. 解答：C

解説 "The network used fake accounts to spread misleading claims that disparaged the safety of the Pfizer and AstraZeneca vaccines."から，Cが正解。

訳例 偽のアカウントは何をしましたか。

A. フェイスブックは役に立たないが，ツイッターは大丈夫と言った。

B. フェイスブックはロシアがファイザー社とアストラゼネカ社の新型コロナウイルス感染症ワクチンを製造したことを証明したと言った。

C. ファイザー社とアストラゼネカ社のワクチンは危険だと主張した。

D. インド，ラテンアメリカ，そして米国が新型コロナウイルス感染症ワクチンのスプートニクVを中傷したと言った。

86. 解答：A

解説 "The fake accounts targeted India, Latin America and the U.S., using several social media platforms including Facebook and Instagram."から，Aが正解。

訳例 ファゼネットワークはどのように中傷キャンペーンを広げましたか。

A. 複数のソーシャルメディア・プラットフォームを利用した。

B. 新聞社に手紙を書いた。

C. 作曲をした。

D. さまざまなワクチンを作った。

87. 解答：B

解説 "That ploy backfired when influencers in Germany and France exposed the network's scheme."から，Bが正解。

訳例 ファゼネットワークはどのように逆効果になりましたか。

A. インフルエンサーがネットワークのオファーを宣伝した。

B. インフルエンサーがネットワークのオファーを暴露した。

C. ネットワークはインフルエンサーへの支払いを拒否した。

D. インフルエンサーはネットワークにもっと支払うように頼んだ。

88. 解答：C

解説 「設定はずさんであまり多くの人に広がらなかったがやり方は巧妙だっ

た」の意味だから，C が正解。

訳例　下線部 (88) “Although it was sloppy and didn’t have very good reach, it was an elaborate setup, ” の意味は何ですか。
A. 最初から最後まで設定が愚かだった。
B. 設定はその目的をすべて達成した。
C. 設定は失敗したが見事だった。
D. 設定は多くの人を有名にした。

89.　解答：B

解説　ファゼはインフルエンサーたちに，報酬を得ていることに触れないよう促し，また，メディアのワクチンに関する報道を批判するよう提案していたので，狡猾《こうかつ》であることから，B が正解。

訳例　ファゼはなぜ「インフルエンサーに，自分たちが報酬を得ていることを言わないように促し，また，メディアのワクチン報道を批判するように勧めた」のでしょうか。
A. ファゼは親切だった。　B. ファゼは狡猾だった。
C. ファゼは混乱していた。　D. ファゼはチンパンジーを怖がった。

90.　解答：D

解説　下線部は，「危険信号が多すぎます」「私はそれをしないことにしました」とフランス人ユーチューバーのレオ・グラッセは AP 通信に語った，と言う意味だから，D が正解。

訳例　グラッセは下線部 (90) “Too many red flags,” French YouTuber Léo Grasset told the Associated Press. “I decided not to do it” で何を意味していますか。
A. グラッセは冒険が好きだった。
B. グラッセはファゼが好きだった。
C. グラッセはロシアが好きだった。
D. グラッセは何かがおかしいと感じた。

訳例　　フェイスブックは，2021 年 8 月 11 日火曜日，ファイザー社とアストラゼネカ社が製造した新型コロナウイルス感染症ワクチンを中傷するためにソーシャルメディアのインフルエンサーにお金を払おうとしたロシアの謎の広告代理店に関連する数百のアカウントを削除したと報告した。65 のフェイスブックのアカウントと 243 のインスタグラムのアカウントのネットワークに，無名のクライアントに代わってロシアで働く広告マーケティング会社のファゼが関与していることがわかった。

そのネットワークは，偽のアカウントを使用して，ファイザー社とアストラゼネカ社のワクチンの安全性を損なうような誤解を招く主張を広めていた。あるものは，アストラゼネカ社の注射は人をチンパンジーに変えてしまうと主張した。偽アカウントは，インド，ラテンアメリカ，米国をターゲットに，フェイスブックやインスタグラムを含む複数のソーシャルメディア・プラットフォームを使用していた。

ロシアは新型コロナウイルス感染症ワクチンのスプートニクVを積極的に海外に売り込んでおり，一部のアナリストは点数稼ぎの努力と見ている。しかし，フェイスブックの代表者は，中傷キャンペーンが行われた背景として考えられる理由について，推測することはしなかった。

ファゼネットワークはまた，いくつかの国のソーシャルメディアのインフルエンサーに，誤解を招く内容を再投稿したらお金を払うという連絡をした。ドイツとフランスのインフルエンサーがこのネットワークの陰謀を暴露したため，この策略は裏目に出た。

フェイスブックは，ファゼのアカウントを削除するとともに，ファゼをそのプラットフォームから追放した。

ファゼの試みは，オンラインではあまり成功せず，いくつかの投稿は1つの反応さえも得ることができなかった。しかし，キャンペーンは失敗したかもしれないが，ソーシャルメディアのインフルエンサーに協力を求めたという点では，注目すべきものである。フェイスブックのセキュリティ・ポリシーの責任者であるナサニエル・グライチャーによると，「ファゼの試みはずさんで，あまり広がらなかったが，手の込んだ設定だった」と彼は言う。

フェイスブックの調査員によると，一部のインフルエンサーは題材を投稿したが，ファゼの仕業に関する話が出始めると，後でそれを削除したという。

ファゼからの申し出は，インフルエンサーたちに，報酬を得ていることに触れないよう促し，また，メディアのワクチンに関する報道を批判するよう提案していた。「危険信号が多すぎます」「私はそれをしないことにしました」とフランス人ユーチューバーのレオ・グラッセはAP通信に語った。

X

まとまりのある会話文を読み，会話が行われている状況におけるイディオム，語彙力，コミュニケーションの力を試す問題。10問出題。

91. 解答：C

解説 “It’s sad. I mean being afraid of people because of COVID-19.” とミナコが述べていることから，Cが正解。

訳例　ジムが買い物から帰ってきたとき，ミナコが悲しんだことは何ですか。

A. 店員がジムに対して無礼だった。

B. 彼は欲しいものが見つからなかった。

C. 新型コロナウイルス感染症に罹《かか》っているかもしれない人を恐れること。
D. ジムはマスクをしていない少年たちに無礼だった。

92.　解答：A

解説　“I mostly miss seeing friends, eating out and going to bookstores.” とジム言い，ミナコも “I agree.” と述べていることから，A が正解。

訳例　ジムとミナコがパンデミックの中で最もできなくて残念に思っていることは何ですか？
A. 友達に会えなくなることや，本屋とレストランに行けなくなること。
B. ダウンタウンのオフィスで働けなくなったこと。
C. 旅行が恋しい。
D. 彼らは満員電車を恋しがっている。

93.　解答：A

解説　“At least we two can do all our work from home via our computers.” とミナコが言い，ジムも “And we get along well together all the time.” と述べていることから，A が正解。

訳例　ジムとミナコはどのような点で幸運なのですか。
A. 家で仕事ができるし，一緒にいるのが好きだ。
B. 彼らはハワイで休暇を取ることができる。
C. 彼らはピザを食べることができる。
D. 彼らはテニスを楽しむことができる。

94.　解答：B

解説　“Sadly, a lot of families that sequester together find out they don’t like each other. Sometimes that leads to domestic violence.” とミナコが述べていることから，B が正解。

訳例　隔離することの悪い面は何ですか。
A. 新型コロナウイルス感染症を逃れたり避けたりできる。
B. 家庭内暴力がある。　C. 友好的な会話。　D. 電車に乗り遅れること。

95.　解答：D

解説　“And we get along well together all the time.” “I feel sorry for the people who go out to have fun and get sick.” とジムが言い，“I feel sorry for restaurants that are losing business because of the pandemic."とミナコが述べているがDについては述べられていないことから，Dが正解。

訳例　ジムとミナコが会話の中で話していないのは誰ですか。
A. 家で仲良くしている人
B. パンデミックにより経営が悪化しているレストラン
C. 遊びに行って新型コロナウイルス感染症に感染する人たち
D. パンデミック時に学校で勉強している学生

96. 解答：A

解説　"If so, I trust our town's progressive mayor will arrange to have the entire town vaccinated."とジムが言い，"It's likely he'll set up a date and time for everyone as he did the first time."とミナコが述べていることから，Aが正解。

訳例　ジムとミナコは，新型コロナウイルス感染症変異株の追加接種のために，どのようなことをしてもらえると期待していますか。
A. 進歩的な市長のこれまでの力量から判断して，非常によくしてもらえる。
B. ものすごく大混乱になる可能性が非常に高い。
C. 高齢者にしか効果がないだろう。
D. 若い人にしか効果がないだろう。

97. 解答：B

解説　"I do miss our favorite pizza restaurant."とミナコが述べていることから，Bが正解。

訳例　パンデミックにおいて，ミナコがとても恋しいと思うものは何ですか。
A. 洋服の買い物　　B. お気に入りのピザ屋さんでの食事
C. マスクを付けること　　D. 自宅で仕事をすること

98. 解答：B

解説　"I feel the same way, but we can't take chances."とジムがミナコの気持ちを的確に「危険を犯すことはできない」と述べていることから，Bが正解。

訳例　ミナコが「友達を裏切っているような気がすることがある」と言うのはなぜですか。
A. 彼女は彼らからお金を盗む。

B. 彼女はピザ屋で食べたいけど，怖くて食べられない。
C. 彼女はもうピザが好きではない。
D. 彼女はピザ屋が閉店することを望んでいる。

99. 解答：C

解説 “Speaking of chances, you’ve lost too much weight, by which I mean muscle.” “We’ll walk in the apartment and try other exercises.” とミナコが述べていることから，C が正解。

訳例 ミナコが気づいた，ジムが隔離されていることに関する問題点は何ですか。
A. 彼は太ってしまったので，食べるのを控えた方がいい。
B. 彼の記憶力は弱くなっている。
C. 彼は体重が減ったので，アパートの中を歩いたり，他の運動をした方がいい。
D. 彼は寝すぎである。

100. 解答：D

解説 ジムとミナコの新型コロナウイルス感染症に関する姿勢は，健康と安全を一番に考えているので，D が正解。

訳例 この話にふさわしいタイトルは何ですか。
A. 隔離は危険　　B. ジムとミナコのお出かけ
C. 新型コロナウイルス感染症は問題ではない　　D. 隔離は必要である

訳例 ジム　：僕らの食料を買いに行ったんだ。男の子のグループがマスクをしていなかったので，ショックだったなぁ。
ミナコ：あなたは，それでどうしたの，ジム？
ジム：　できるだけ早く彼らから離れたんだ。
ミナコ：悲しいわね。新型コロナウイルス感染症のせいで人を怖がっているなんて。
ジム：　そうなんだ，とても悲しいね。友達に会ったり，外食したり，本屋に行ったりするのができないのがいちばん寂しいな。
ミナコ：私もそう思うの。少なくとも私たち２人は，家でパソコンを使ってすべての仕事ができるわ。
ジム：　それに，僕たちはいつも仲良くやっているし。
ミナコ：悲しいことに，一緒に隔離している多くの家族が，お互い嫌いだということに気がつくの。それが家庭内暴力につながることもあるのよ。
ジム：　そして，家から逃げ出してウイルスに感染する人もいるんだ。

ミナコ：パンデミックのせいで商売が成り立たなくなっているレストランが気の毒だわ。

ジム　：遊びに行って病気になる人たちが哀れだね。

ミナコ：新型コロナウイルス感染症の新しい変異株ができたの。私たちの注射が効くといいんだけど。追加接種が必要だと思うわ。

ジム：　もしそうなら，僕たちの町の進歩的な市長が，町全体に予防接種を受けられるように手配してくれると信じているよ。

ミナコ：最初のときと同じように，みんなのために日時を決めてくれると思うわ。

ジム：　正直に言ってね。外食や洋服の買い物が恋しくならない？

ミナコ：うーん，それほどでもないわ。お気に入りのピザ屋さんが恋しくなることはあるの。そこで食べないと，友達を裏切っているような気になることがあるわ。

ジム：　僕も同じ気持ちだけど，危ないことをするわけにはいかないよ。

ミナコ：そうね。チャンスといえば，あなたは体重，つまり筋肉が減りすぎたわ。

ジム：　そうだね。その通りだ。

ミナコ：アパートの中を歩いたり，他の運動もやってみましょう。

2021年C級第2回試験　正解一覧

Ⅰ

1. C　2. A　3. D　4. A　5. B　6. D　7. A　8. B　9. D　10. B

Ⅱ

11. B　12. A　13. D　14. C　15. B　16. A　17. A　18. B　19. B　20. C

Ⅲ

21. B　22. D　23. A　24. A　25. D　26. B　27. D　28. A　29. A　30. C

Ⅳ

31. C　32. B　33. A　34. C　35. A　36. C　37. B　38. D　39. C　40. D

Ⅴ

41. C　42. B　43. C　44. D　45. C　46. A　47. B　48. A　49. D　50. D

Ⅵ

51. C　52. A　53. B　54. C　55. B　56. D　57. A　58. C　59. C　60. B

Ⅶ

61. C　62. B　63. A　64. C　65. B　66. A　67. D　68. C　69. D　70. C

Ⅷ

71. D　72. B　73. C　74. A　75. B　76. A　77. C　78. B　79. D　80. D

Ⅸ

81. C　82. A　83. D　84. D　85. C　86. A　87. B　88. C　89. B　90. D

Ⅹ

91. C　92. A　93. A　94. B　95. D　96. A　97. B　98. B　99. C　100. D

2022年

第1回試験

問題

C級試験問題用紙

C級

外務省後援

２０２２年度第１回国際連合公用語

英語検定試験（100分）

受験上の注意

1．問題用紙は試験開始の合図があるまで開いてはいけません。その間に、この**受験上の注意を熟読**しておいてください。

2．**受験番号と氏名を解答用紙（マークシート）**に記入してください。

3．解答用紙の配布は１人１部のみです。複数の配布は致しません。

4．試験開始前は、答案への解答記入は禁止です。

5．マークシートの記入は、必ずＨＢ以上の濃い鉛筆を使って該当箇所を黒く塗りつぶしてください。書き間違いの場合は「アト」が残らないように消してください。マークシートは絶対に折ったり曲げたりしないでください。

6．受験級、受験地区、会場番号、受験番号のマークシートへの記入は監督者の指示に従い、間違いなく記入してください。**(裏表紙の「マークシート記入例」参照)**

7．試験問題についての質問は、印刷が不鮮明な場合を除き、一切受けつけません。

8．中途退室の際は、マークシートを監督者に渡し、他の受験者の迷惑にならないように静かに退室してください。中途退室後の再入室はできません。

9．試験中は他の受験者の妨げとなる行動は慎んでください。また携帯電話等の電源はお切りください。

10．マークシートは監督者に提出し、問題用紙はご自由にお持ち帰りください。

＊試験問題の複製や転載、インターネットへのアップロード等、いかなる媒体への転用を禁止します。

リスニングテストについて

1．リスニングテストは試験開始後、合図があってから実施されます。(40問あります)

2．リスニングテストが始まる前にリスニング問題の指示と内容を読んで、どういう形式のテストなのか、概要をつかんでおいてください。

3．テスト中の発言は、放送機器の具合が悪く放送された英語の聴き取りができない場合を除いて、しないようにしてください。

試験結果について

1．試験の結果は2022年6月29日㈬頃に通知します。

2．その間に住所変更をされた方は、郵便局へ住所変更の届け出を忘れずに行ってください。

3．発表前の試験結果のお問合せには応じられません。

UNA-JAPAN
公益財団法人 日本国際連合協会
http://www.unaj.or.jp/

I．これから短い英文を10言います。英文は２回言います。よく聞いて、会話が成り立つように最も適切なものをA、B、C、Dの中から１つ選びなさい。途中でメモを取ってもかまいません。

1. A. I'm sorry you are still sick.
B. Do you miss me that much?
C. Enjoy yourself but be careful.
D. You should call the doctor.

2. A. I'll assist you.
B. I'm glad you can use it.
C. You know what you're doing.
D. Thank you for the present.

3. A. I bought the book yesterday.
B. They sell books downtown.
C. It's on your bed.
D. It's a very interesting book.

4. A. I'm hungry.
B. It would be pretty much the same.
C. You should not change your life.
D. I need to change into a suit.

5. A. I'd love to go there.
B. There is a fast train to Nagoya.
C. There is a strike in Canada.
D. Thank you! I'd love to be in Europe.

6. A. Yes! I'll have the chicken special tonight.
B. No, I do not care for sashimi.
C. I'll have the special since I don't like beef.
D. I'll have vegetables with my roast beef.

7. A. The meeting is at four in the afternoon.
B. There was not enough of a majority.
C. The meeting went very well.
D. The president is popular.

8. A. I'm glad we brought our lunch.
B. Don't worry about the cat.
C. We are where we should be.
D. The car needs gas.

9. A. I also dislike summer.
B. We'll go snowboarding then.
C. I love to watch the leaves turn colors.
D. I'll take out my surfboard.

10. A. Yes, it is nice to go swimming.
B. I just got a booster shot.
C. I have a beautiful garden.
D. We must buy a new house.

II. これから短い会話を10言います。会話は２回繰り返します。そのあと、会話の内容について10の質問をします。質問も２回繰り返します。よく聞いて、それぞれの質問の答えとして最も適切なものをA、B、C、Dの中から１つ選びなさい。途中でメモを取ってもかまいません。

11. A. Don't worry about not wearing a mask.
B. I'm glad we're staying home today.
C. Wear a mask only at home.
D. It's important to wear a mask outside.

12. A. The woman talks too much on the telephone.
B. The telephone caller has good reasons to talk.
C. The man does not talk much on the telephone.
D. The woman is a friend of the telephone caller.

13. A. He'll contact her as time permits.
B. She'll call him until she gets him.
C. She'll find the best time to call him.
D. He'll call just before coming home.

14. A. He'll drive her to the highway.
B. He'll ask someone to help her.
C. He'll help her find her way.
D. He'll tell her where his house is.

15. A. She saw who stole his car.
B. His car was only moved.
C. His car is where he parked it.
D. Someone is driving his car away.

16. A. He hates getting shots.
B. If others get shots, he doesn't need to.
C. He has not yet gotten a booster shot.
D. He also got a booster shot.

17. A. She thought it was interesting.
B. She missed it.
C. She knows what the story is about.
D. She saw it later.

18. A. He owns a good restaurant.
B. He thinks he knows a hotel.
C. He seems to know many good department stores.
D. He thinks highly of Kobe's international restaurants.

19. A. She'll give him a ride.
B. She will lend him some money.
C. He will help her.
D. She can't help me.

20. A. He's retired to Paris.
B. He has lived in Paris off and on.
C. He has moved a lot.
D. He's working in Paris.

Ⅲ. これから英文を２回繰り返します。そのあと、内容について10の質問をします。質問も２回繰り返します。よく聞いて、それぞれの質問の答えとして最も適切なものをA、B、C、Dの中から１つ選びなさい。途中でメモを取ってもかまいません。

21. A. It was hot.
B. It was cloudy.
C. It was raining.
D. It was sunny.

22. A. It probably had a home.
B. It was obviously abandoned.
C. It was dangerous.
D. It was quiet.

23. A. He put it inside his jacket.
B. He put it on his shoulder.
C. He fed it.
D. He gave it away.

24. A. He was angry.
B. He was happy.
C. He was sleepy.
D. He was worried.

25. A. Go outside.
B. Take a hot bath.
C. Eat dinner.
D. Go to bed.

26. A. A kitten.
B. A puppy.
C. A coin.
D. A towel.

27. A. To find another home for it. B. To put it in a cage.
C. To keep it. D. To lend it to friends.

28. A. It cried all the time. B. It bit and scratched.
C. It stayed out all the time. D. It never went outside.

29. A. It cried. B. It scratched them.
C. It bit them. D. All of the above.

30. A. It was hungry. B. It wanted to go outside.
C. It sensed the gas leak. D. It was lonely.

Ⅳ. これから会話を２回繰り返します。そのあと、内容について10の質問をします。質問も２回繰り返します。よく聞いて、それぞれの質問の答えとして最も適切なものをA、B、C、Dの中から１つ選びなさい。途中でメモを取ってもかまいません。

Yuki and Joe are talking.

31. A. Dull and common.
B. Vivid and unique.
C. Nice but not exciting.
D. Joe doesn't understand women's clothing.

32. A. Yuki did. B. A company did.
C. Her dressmaker did. D. Joe did.

33. A. Her mother. B. A dressmaker.
C. No one. D. Joe.

34. A. Africa. B. Japan.
C. Europe. D. Australia.

35. A. Never. B. possibly.
C. Yes. D. Only for festivals.

36. A. They are very comfortable especially in spring and summer.
B. They are best worn in winter.
C. Autumn is when they are most comfortable.
D. The dressmaker makes them comfortable for all seasons.

37. A. Go drinking.
B. Eat at a vegetarian restaurant.
C. Eat fish.
D. Eat meat.

38. A. She throws them away.
B. She give them to poor people.
C. She gives them to recycling.
D. She changes old clothes into new clothes.

39. A. Zambia. B. South Africa.
C. Ethiopia. D. It does not say.

40. A. Clothes for Movie Stars
B. How to Get Rid of Old Clothes
C. The Exceptional Dressmaker
D. Why Vegetarian Food is Good for You

V. 次の英文の下線部の意味を最もよく表す語または語句をA、B、C、Dの中から1つ選びなさい。

41. **They are at each other's throats.**
A. are good friends B. hate each other
C. are in love with each other D. don't know each other

42. **She expressed her point of view very well.**
A. ideas B. pictures
C. presents D. greetings

43. **He looks up to the President.**
A. trains B. imitates
C. disdains D. admires

44. **Can you make out the poem's meaning?**
A. paint B. understand
C. advertise D. bury

45. **She counts on you.**
A. accepts B. feels for
C. relies on D. lives with

46. He <u>lost face</u> before the audience.

A. was humiliated
B. won a point
C. got the answer
D. did not feel well

47. He <u>can't help but</u> speak loudly.

A. is willing to
B. only knows how to
C. needs help to
D. refuses to

48. I <u>lost faith in</u> the leader.

A. liked
B. hated
C. was indifferent to
D. was disappointed with

49. I was <u>moved</u> by her kindness.

A. brokenhearted
B. impressed
C. disgusted
D. bored

50. His piano is improving <u>stage by stage</u>.

A. quickly
B. perfectly
C. little by little
D. not at all

Ⅵ. 次の英文を読み、設問の答えとして最も適切なものをA、B、C、Dの中から1つ選びなさい。

The establishment of the Peacebuilding Commission (PBC) was proposed during the World Summit of the United Nations in 2005. The United Nations not only helps to end conflicts, but also plays a role in preventing conflict-affected countries (or regions) from *relapsing into civil war. To promote "sustaining peace," the Commission takes a consistent approach to making suggestions and proposals on comprehensive strategies for the post-conflict process of peacebuilding and *restoration from conflict resolution to *restoration, and from *reintegration to *reconstruction.

The Peacebuilding Commission is an *intergovernmental *advisory body composed of 31 Member States elected from the General Assembly, the Security Council, and the Economic and Social Council. Within the United Nations System, the Peacebuilding Commission is an *unprecedented organization in that its *mandate includes the authority to provide advice to the Security Council, the General Assembly and the Economic and Social Council on critical issues of peacebuilding. The United Nations has established the Peacebuilding Architecture, which consists of not only the Peacebuilding Commission, but also the Peacebuilding Support Office (PBSO) and the Peacebuilding Fund (PBF). This architecture of three new bodies was added to thc United Nations System in 2005-2006 to strengthen efforts to help post-conflict countries to build sustainable peace and prevent *relapse into violent conflict.

Security Council Resolution 2282 of 2016 *reaffirms that the Peacebuilding Commission has a number of important missions, including bringing sustained international attention to sustaining peace as well as serving as a platform to *convene all *relevant actors within and outside the United Nations, including those from Member States, national authorities, United Nations missions and country teams, international, regional and sub-regional organizations, international financial institutions, civil society, women's groups, youth organizations and, where *relevant, the private sector and national human rights institutions.

Many meetings of the Peacebuilding Commission are held at the Trusteeship Council Chamber. The Trusteeship Council deliberated the administration and supervision of the trust territories, including those *detached from enemy states as a result of the Second World War. In November 1994, the Council (60) suspended its work following the independence of Palau, the last UN trust territory.

注）*relapse 再び陥る、再発する　*restoration 復旧、復興
*reintegration 社会復帰　*reconstruction 復興
*intergovernmental 政府間の　*advisory body 諮問機関
*unprecedented 前例のない　*mandate 権限
*reaffirm 繰り返し強調する　*convene を招集する
*relevant 関連がある　*detached 分離した

51. What was the organization that proposed the establishment of the Peacebuilding Commission?

A. The General Assembly.
B. The Trusteeship Council.
C. The World Summit of the United Nations.
D. The Economic and Social Council.

52. What is one of the roles of the United Nations according to the text?

A. To prevent conflicts from relapsing into civil war.
B. To strengthen one powerful country.
C. To promote the United Nations interests.
D. To exclude women's groups.

53. Which of the following is NOT true regarding the Peacebuilding Commission's job according to the text?

A. It promotes "sustaining peace."

B. It makes suggestions and proposals on a single strategy for peacebuilding.

C. Its purpose supports the post-conflict process of peacebuilding and restoration.

D. Its strategies range from conflict resolution to restoration, and from reintegration to reconstruction.

54. How are the 31 Member States of the Peacebuilding Commission decided?

A. Through appointment of the General Assembly.

B. Through election by the General Assembly, the Security Council and the Economic and Social Council.

C. Through nomination from the trust territories.

D. Through election from conflict-affected countries.

55. What is particular about the Peacebuilding Commission?

A. It must follow the order by the General Assembly, the Security Council and the Economic and Social Council.

B. The General Assembly, the Security Council and the Economic and Social Council give advice to the Peacebuilding Commission.

C. It has the authority to provide advice to the General Assembly, the Security Council and the Economic and Social Council on critical issues of peacebuilding.

D. It avoids its mandate to provide advice to the General Assembly, the Security Council and the Economic and Social Council on critical issues of peacebuilding.

56. What are the three bodies that consist of the Peacebuilding Architecture?

A. The Peacebuilding Commission, the Peacebuilding Support Office and the Peacebuilding Fund.

B. The General Assembly, international financial institutions and youth organizations.

C. The Trusteeship Council, women's groups and regional organizations.

D. The General Assembly, the Security Council and the Economic and Social Council.

57. **What was the purpose of the Peacebuilding Architecture being added to the United Nations System?**

A. To strengthen concentrated political power from developing into conflict.

B. To hire more employees to work for the Peacebuilding Architecture.

C. To give more authority to provide advice to the General Assembly, the Security Council and the Economic and Social Council.

D. To strengthen efforts to help post-conflict countries to build sustainable peace and prevent relapse into violent conflict.

58. **Which of the following is NOT true regarding the Peacebuilding Commission's missions according to the text?**

A. Bringing sustained international attention to sustaining peace.

B. Relevant actors to convene outside the United Nations include international, regional and sub-regional organizations.

C. Serving as a platform to convene all relevant actors only outside the United Nations.

D. Relevant actors to convene outside the United Nations include civil society, women's groups, youth organizations and, where relevant, the private sector and national human rights institutions.

59. **What did the Trusteeship Council deliberate?**

A. Administration of the independent countries.

B. Supervision of the conflict-affected countries.

C. Administration and supervision of the post-conflict countries.

D. Administration and supervision of the trust territories.

60. **What does the underlined part (60) suspended mean?**

A. forced

B. expanded

C. exchanged

D. stopped

Ⅶ. 次の各組の文の空所には同じ語が入ります。最も適切なものをA、B、C、Dの中から1つ選びなさい。

61. **I like this _________ because of its design. Don't _________ him as a liar.**

A. maker　B. brand　C. instrument　D. client

62. **I must _________ him. It's a _________ to be home.**

A. comfort　B. seat　C. cry　D. problem

63. **I paid an ________ of $100. He ate to ________.**

A. effort B. interest C. over D. excess

64. **She will ________ down a taxi. I saw their ________ on the ship.**

A. captain B. catch C. flag D. discover

65. **You can ________ on him. She is very ________.**

A. lean B. jump C. stable D. beg

66. **Don't ________ it. He deserves ________.**

A. punish B. harbor C. mystery D. mention

67. **I like this ________ cooker. He's getting a lot of ________.**

A. tin B. pressure C. damage D. pull

68. **She speaks French like a ________. This tree is ________ to Australia.**

A. native B. nation C. citizen D. tower

69. **The boy is going through a ________. We will ________ out the rules.**

A. crisis B. phase C. change D. decrease

70. **We must ________ out our clothing. He is a good ________.**

A. conclude B. strain C. sort D. blow

Ⅷ. 次のA、B、C、Dからなる各組の英文には下線部に誤りを含むものが1つあります。その文を選びなさい。

71. A. She is making a raft using logs.

B. You need to log in to the computer.

C. His trip was logged at the computer.

D. He slept like a log last night.

72. A. What fun!

B. She does not like to make fun of people.

C. Have a fun!

D. He had a fun time at the zoo.

73. A. I'll come to your wedding party rains or shines.
B. It rains a lot in winter.
C. The picnic was rained out.
D. I need a rain check on your dinner party.

74. A. The train ticket is good to a whole day.
B. The tennis player has a good chance to win the game.
C. She wants to live in her hometown for good.
D. Please behave for your own good.

75. A. She teaches at a junior college.
B. Please teach me how to get to the station.
C. He taught me how to drive.
D. She taught him a lesson he never forgot.

76. A. She is talented in more ways than one.
B. He met his old friend on his way to school.
C. There was a broken-down truck at the way.
D. She went to see her sister all the way to New York.

77. A. They are a love match.
B. The pearl necklace matches her dress.
C. She won the tennis match last night.
D. The baseball players are equally match.

78. A. He lives in a nursing home.
B. New Orleans is home of jazz.
C. She is interested in home economics.
D. He was at home when the package was delivered.

79. A. The prices are going up higher and higher.
B. She is more an artist than a teacher.
C. I will not see him anymore.
D. The more I thought about my holiday, more happy I became.

80. A. She showed me around her house.
B. He doesn't like to show off his fortune.
C. It goes to show food is important for your health.
D. I waited for him, but he didn't show on.

Ⅸ. 次の英文を読み、設問の答として最も適切なものをA、B、C、Dの中から１つ選びなさい。

Russia's *shelling of Chernobyl's nuclear power plant in Ukraine sparked a fire at one of its six *reactors, stirring fears of a 1986-like *meltdown.

Ukrainian workers extinguished the fire. But there was damage to the reactor *compartment. The International Atomic Energy Agency (IAEA) warned that war in and around such nuclear facilities presents extreme risks.

Ukraine's state *nuclear regulator warned that if fighting interrupts power supply to the nuclear plant, it would be forced to use less-reliable *diesel generators to provide emergency power to operating cooling systems. A failure of those systems could lead to a meltdown disaster similar to that of Japan's Fukushima plant.

Ukrainian President, Volodymyr Zelenskyy, declared in the middle of the night, "If there is an explosion, that's the end of everyone. The end of Europe." He called for an end to fighting near the plant.

The reactor that was hit was *offline, but it still contains highly *radioactive nuclear fuel. Four of the other six reactors have now been taken offline, leaving only one in operation.

Perhaps the biggest concern is the plant's electrical power supply. One expert said that the loss of *off-site electrical power could force the plant to rely on emergency diesel generators, which are highly unreliable and could fail or run out of fuel, causing a station *blackout that would stop the water circulation needed to cool the spent fuel pool.

Ukraine is heavily reliant on nuclear energy, with 15 reactors at four stations that provide about half the country's electricity.

In an appeal to the IAEA for help, Ukrainian officials said that the Chernobyl staff have been held by the Russian military without *rotation and are *exhausted. Ukraine appealed to Russia to let the regular Ukrainian Chernobyl staff "do their job safely and effectively."

During *warfare, the danger of a meltdown becomes more likely.

注）*shelling 爆撃　*reactor 原子炉　*meltdown （原子炉の）炉心溶解
*compartment 仕切った部分　*nuclear regulator 原子力規制当局
*diesel generator ディーゼル発電機　*offline 稼働していない
*radioactive 放射性の　*off-site 外部の、現地から離れた
*blackout 停電　*rotation 交替　*exhausted 疲れ切った、へとへとの
*warfare 戦争状態

81. What are the "stirring fears" at Chernobyl's nuclear power plant?

A. Russian shelling.

B. Fire in one of reactors.

C. Fear of a meltdown.

D. All of the above.

82. What "presents extreme risks" to the nuclear power plant?

A. It is too old.

B. Lack of spare parts.

C. War near the plant.

D. Up-to-date technology.

83. What would happen if the Chernobyl reactor went into a meltdown?

A. Nothing at all.

B. A disaster like the Fukushima plant.

C. Only minor problems.

D. The Chernobyl nuclear power plant will start working again.

84. What did Ukrainian President Volodymyr Zelenskyy say about Chernobyl?

A. "Go back to sleep. Nothing to worry about."

B. "I'll talk to Putin. He'll help us."

C. "If there is an explosion, that's the end of everyone. The end of Europe."

D. "It will destroy the Russian Army. No more war."

85. What did Zelenskyy call for?

A. An end to fighting around the Chernobyl nuclear power plant.

B. Encouraging Ukrainians to attack the Russians.

C. To get out of Kiev immediately.

D. To not to worry about Chernobyl.

86. What is the worst problem with the Chernobyl reactor right now?

A. Nuclear explosions inside the Chernobyl reactors.

B. Russians leaving the Chernobyl nuclear power plant.

C. Unreliable diesel power generators could fail or run out of fuel.

D. Ukrainians attacking Russia.

87. What energy issue does Ukraine have to face?

A. It has only one nuclear power plant.

B. It has no nuclear power plants.

C. It is heavily dependent on nuclear power.

D. It is heavily dependent on solar power.

88. What is the appeal for help to the IAEA about?

A. The Chernobyl staff are being held by the Russian military.

B. The Chernobyl staff have not been rotated and are exhausted.

C. The Russian military should let the Chernobyl staff work safely and effectively.

D. All of the above.

89. What makes the danger of a meltdown more likely at the Chernobyl plant?

A. Peace.

B. Warfare.

C. Bad weather.

D. All of the above.

90. What is the best title for this story?

A. The Problem with Chernobyl is Minor

B. War and Danger to Chernobyl

C. Terrible Explosions are Rocking Chernobyl

D. Sightseeing Tours at Chernobyl

X. 次の会話を読み、設問の答として最も適切なものをA、B、C、Dの中から１つ選びなさい。

Gina : Hi Jiro! I'm glad to see you! I missed you! How are you?

Jiro : I've barely left my apartment. I really missed you so much!

Gina : What have you been doing?

Jiro : I have *sequestered myself—but not only because of the pandemic. My back has been in terrible shape for over two weeks. I need to get to the doctor at my hospital, but I am in too much pain. Also, the buses are crowded and there is the danger of COVID-19.

Gina : I have a car now. I'll take you to the hospital right away.

Jiro : Thank you! I'll call my doctor and see if him can take me. [Calling.] Can you see me about my bad back? You can! Great! Thank you, doctor.

Gina : That's good luck. Can you walk? My car is not far.

Jiro : I can. I have a walking stick from when I used to go hiking.

Gina : By the way, you look thinner. How did you lose weight?

Jiro : I have not eaten fast food for two weeks. Maybe that's how I did it.

Gina : Did you cook for yourself?

Jiro : I was not good at cooking, but during my *sequestration I learned how to cook through the Internet. Now I can cook pretty well for myself.

Gina : That's great!

Jiro : Not only that, I got interested in organic food and started to cook better. I found an Internet site that delivers packages of organic eggs, fruits, vegetables, and meat.

Gina : That must be especially convenient for you since you have a bad back.

Jiro : Exactly right! And on top of that, I have found organic foods taste better and are better for your health.

Gina : After we see your doctor, I'll take you home in my car. Then I'll do some shopping for you. There are other things you need for your apartment.

Jiro : I cannot thank you enough!

注) *sequester 隔離する　*sequestration 隔離

91. Why do Gina and Jiro miss each other so much?

A. They are boyfriend and girlfriend.

B. They are brother and sister.

C. They are not friends.

D. It does not say.

92. Why was Jiro at home?

A. Only because of the pandemic.

B. He was very busy writing a long report.

C. Only because of his back pain.

D. Because of the pandemic and his back pain.

93. Where will Gina first take Jiro?

A. To a doctor.　B. To her home for dinner.

C. To a restaurant.　D. To shop.

94. What does Gina notice about Jiro?

A. His voice has changed.　B. He has lost weight.

C. He is dizzy.　D. He is wearing glasses.

95. What has Jiro not eaten for two weeks?

A. Stew.　B. Sushi.

C. Organic food.　D. Fast food.

96. Is Jiro a good cook?

A. He is a famous cook.
B. He is not a bad cook.
C. It does not say.
D. He is a hopelessly bad cook.

97. What did Jiro discover during his sequestration?

A. Cooking.
B. Medicine.
C. Cycling.
D. How to gain weight.

98. How did Jiro do his grocery shopping during his sequestration?

A. Going to a supermarket.
B. Ordering fast food.
C. Shopping through the Internet.
D. Buying food from a local store.

99. When they finish with the doctor, what will Jiro and Gina do?

A. Jiro will go shopping with Gina.
B. They will take a taxi to the supermarket.
C. Gina will take Jiro home and then go shopping.
D. They will go eat fast food.

100. What is the best title for this conversation?

A. Eating Fast Food
B. Gina to the Rescue!
C. Fun, Fun, Fun During the Pandemic
D. Cooking with Gina

マークシート記入例

東京の本会場でC級を受験する、国連 太郎さん、受験番号が「東京01-40001」、生年月日が「1980年10月24日」の場合の記入例です。

【受験番号/氏名】
それぞれ受験票の記載通りに記入してください。

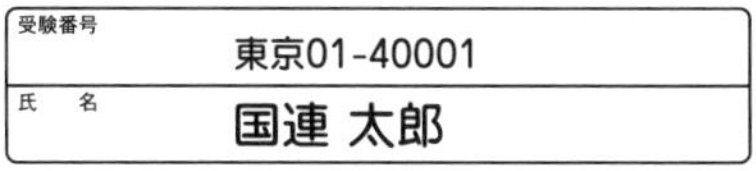

【受験地区】
下段の都道府県部分を塗りつぶしてください。

【会場番号】
都道府県部分に続く２桁の数字を塗りつぶしてください。

【受験番号】
ハイフン（－）以降の５桁の数字を塗りつぶしてください。

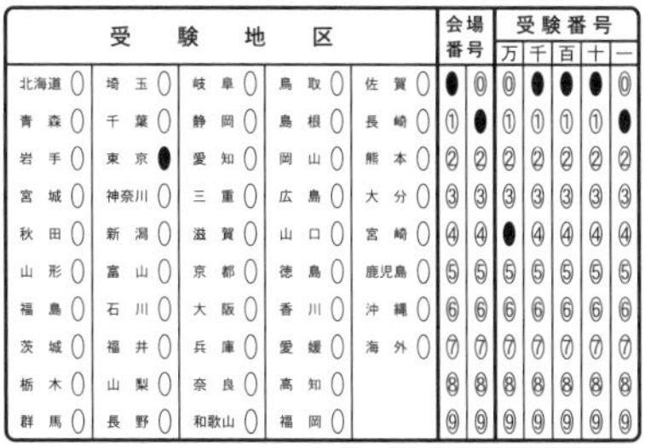

【受験級】
「C」と記入し、下段のC級部分を塗りつぶしてください。

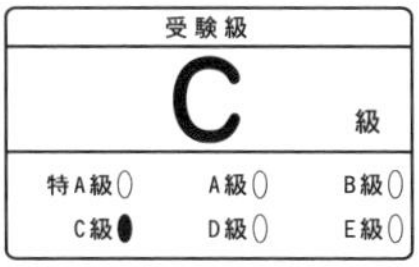

【生年月日】
４桁の西暦・月・日を塗りつぶしてください。
10未満の月・日の十の位は、「０」を塗りつぶしてください。

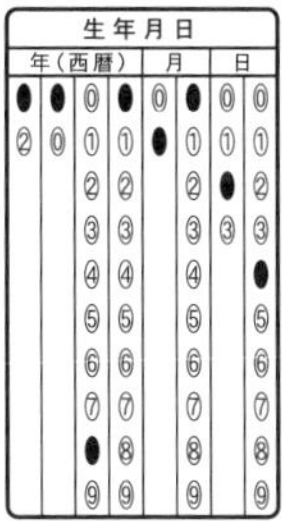

※HB以上の鉛筆を用いてマークをしてください。

※他の地区から会場を変更して受験する場合でも、受験票に記載されている受験地区・会場番号をマークしてください。

2022年
第1回試験
解答・解説

2022年　国連英検C級第1回試験
解答・解説

I　短い英文を2度聴いたあと，
その英文に対して適切な応答を選ぶリスニングテスト。10問出題。

1.　解答：C

解説　話者は相手に長い闘病生活を経て楽しむことができるようになったと伝えているので，選択肢の中で最もふさわしい応答は，Cが正解。

ナレーション　After my long illness I am ready to go out and have fun.
「長い闘病生活の後，私は外に出て楽しむことができるようになりました」

A. まだ具合が悪いんだね。
B. そんなに私がいなくて寂しいですか。
C. 楽しんでください。でも，気をつけてね。
D. お医者さんに電話してください。

2.　解答：A

解説　話者は相手に新しいコンピュータの使い方を尋ねているので，選択肢の中で最もふさわしい応答は，Aが正解。

ナレーション　I bought a new computer, but how can I use it?
「新しいパソコンを買ったけど，どうやって使ったらいいの？」

A. 私がお手伝いします。
B. 使っていただけるとうれしいです。
C. 自分が何をやっているのかわかっているでしょう。
D. プレゼントをありがとうございました。

3.　解答：C

解説　話者は相手に自分の本がある場所を尋ねているので，選択肢の中で最もふさわしい応答は，Cが正解。

ナレーション　Do you know where my book is?

「私の本がどこにあるか知っていますか」

A. 昨日，その本を買いました。　B. 繁華街で本を売っています。

C. それはベッドの上にあります。　D. それはとても面白い本です。

4. 解答：B

解説　話者は相手に人生をどう変えるのか尋ねているので，選択肢の中で最もふさわしい応答は，Bが正解。

ナレーション　How would you change your life?

「あなたなら，人生をどのように変えますか」

A. お腹が空いたよ。　B. それはほとんど同じでしょう。

C. あなたは生活を変えないほうがいい。

D. 私はスーツに着替えなければならない。

5. 解答：A

解説　話者は相手にニュージーランドに行きたいかどうか尋ねているので，選択肢の中で最もふさわしい応答は，Aが正解。

ナレーション　Do you want to go to New Zealand for Christmas?

「クリスマスにニュージーランドに行きたいですか」

A. ぜひ行ってみたいです。

B. 名古屋まで快速電車があります。

C. カナダでストライキがあります。

D. ありがとう。ヨーロッパに行きたいです。

6. 解答：D

解説　話者は相手にローストビーフスペシャルを食べたいかどうか尋ねているので，選択肢の中で最もふさわしい応答は，Dが正解。

ナレーション　Would you like our roast beef special tonight?

「今夜の特製ローストビーフはいかがでしょうか」

A. そうしましょう！　今夜はチキンスペシャルを食べます。

B. いいえ，私は刺身が好きではありません。

C. 牛肉は嫌いなので，スペシャルを食べます。

D. ローストビーフと一緒に野菜を食べます。

7.　解答：B

解説　話者は相手に会議を中止した理由を尋ねているので，選択肢の中で最もふさわしい応答は，B が正解。

ナレーション　Why did the president cancel the meeting?

「なぜ社長は会議を中止したのですか」

A. 会議は午後 4 時からです。　B. 過半数に満たなかった。

C. 会議はとてもうまくいった。　D. 社長は人気がある。

8.　解答：C

解説　話者は相手に道に迷ったのかどうか尋ねているので，選択肢の中で最もふさわしい応答は，C が正解。

ナレーション　Where are we? Are we lost?

「ここはどこなの？　道に迷ったのかしら」

A. 昼食を持って来てよかった。　B. 猫のことは気にしないでください。

C. 私たちはいるべきところにいる。　D. 車はガソリンが必要だ。

9.　解答：D

解説　話者は相手に早く夏が来て欲しい気持ちを伝えているので，選択肢の中で最もふさわしい応答は，D が正解。

ナレーション　I can’t wait until summer comes.

「夏が来るのが待ち遠しいです」

A. 私も夏が嫌いです。

B. じゃあ，スノーボードに行こうよ。

C. 私は紅葉を見るのが好きです。

D. 私はサーフボードを出しておきましょう。

10.　解答：B

解説　話者は相手にパンデミックのため世界が打撃を受けていると伝えているので，選択肢の中で最もふさわしい応答は，B が正解。

ナレーション　The global pandemic has hurt the world.

「世界的なパンデミックのため，世界中が打撃を受けた」

A. はい，泳ぎに行くのはいいですね。

B. 私は追加接種をしたところです。

C. 私は美しい庭を持っています。

D. 私たちは新しい家を買わなければなりません。

II 短い会話を２度聴いたあと，
その内容に関する質問を聴いて答えるリスニングテスト。10 問出題。

11. 解答：D

解説 女性は男性にマスクをするのを忘れていると言っている。D が正解。

A. マスクをしていなくても心配ない。

B. きょうは家にいるのでよかったわ。

C. マスクをするのは家の中だけにしてください。

D. 外ではマスクをすることが大切だ。

ナレーション

Man: Am I forgetting to wear something?

Woman: Your mask!

Question What does the woman mean?

(男)：僕，何か身に着けるもの忘れてないかな？

(女)：あなたのマスク！

質問 女性は何と言っていますか。

12. 解答：B

解説 男性は女性に電話をかけてきた人は，電話で伝えることがあると言っている。B が正解。

A. 女性は電話でしゃべりすぎる。

B. 電話をかけてきた人が話すのはそれなりの理由がある。

C. 男性は電話であまり話さない。

D. 女性は電話をかけてきた人の友人である。

ナレーション

Woman: Your friend talks too much on the telephone.

Man: He seriously needs to talk with someone now.

Question What does the man mean?

(女)：あなたの友達は電話で話しすぎよ。

(男)：彼はいま，誰かと真剣に話す必要があるんだ。

質問 男性は何と言っていますか。

13.　解答：A

解説　女性は男性がニューヨークに着いて時間ができたら電話をして欲しいと言っている。as time permits は「都合のいい時に」の意味。A が正解。

A. 彼は都合のいい時に，彼女に連絡するだろう。

B. 彼女は彼が電話に出るまで電話するだろう。

C. 彼女は彼に電話するのに最適な時間を見つけるだろう。

D. 彼は帰宅する直前に電話をかけるだろう。

ナレーション

Man:　I'll have to get to New York in a hurry.

Woman: Call me when you have the time.

Question　What does the woman mean?

(男)：急いでニューヨークまで行かなくてはならないんだ。

(女)：時間ができたら電話してね。

質問　女性は何と言っていますか。

14.　解答：C

解説　男性は道に迷わないように女性に地図をあげて手伝うと伝えている。C が正解。

A. 彼は彼女を高速道路まで送ってくれるだろう。

B. 彼は誰かに彼女を助けてくれるよう頼むでしょう。

C. 彼は彼女が道を見つけるのを手伝うだろう。

D. 彼は彼女に自分の家がどこにあるか教えるだろう。

ナレーション

Woman: I've lost my way to the highway.

Man:　I'll give you a good map.

Question　What does the man mean?

(女)：高速道路に行くのに迷ってしまいました。

(男)：いい地図をあげるよ。

質問　男性は何と言っていますか。

15.　解答：C

解説　女性は男性の車は駐車した場所にあると言っている。C が正解。

A. 彼女は彼の車を盗んだ人を見た。

B. 彼の車は移動させただけだった。

C. 彼の車は彼が駐車した場所にある。

D. 誰かが彼の車を運転している。

ナレーション

Man: Someone stole my car!

Woman: No, look! It's where you parked it.

Question What does the woman mean?

(男)：誰かが僕の車を盗んだ！

(女)：いいえ，見て！　あなたが駐車した場所にあるわ。

質問　女性は何と言っていますか。

16. 解答：D

解説 男性は女性に追加接種を受けたと言っている。D が正解。

A. 彼は注射を打たれるのが嫌です。

B. 他の人が注射を打っても，彼は打たなくていい。

C. 彼はまだ追加接種を受けたことがない。

D. 彼も追加接種を受けた。

ナレーション

Woman: I'm so happy I finally got my booster shot!

Man: Me too.

Question What does the man mean?

(女)：やっと追加接種が受けられてよかったわ！

(男)：僕もだよ。

質問　男性は何と言っていますか。

17. 解答：B

解説 Oh, dear! は「しまった」の意味なので女性は男性に特別番組を見逃したと伝えている。B が正解。

A. 彼女はそれを面白いと思った。　B. 彼女はそれを逃した。

C. 彼女は話の内容を知っている。　D. 彼女は後でそれを見た。

ナレーション

Man: Did you see that TV special last night?

Woman: Last night? Oh dear!

Question　What does the woman mean?

(男)：昨夜，テレビであの特別番組を見た？

(女)：昨夜，あら，しまった。

質問　女性は何と言っていますか。

18. 解答：D

解説 男性は女性に神戸には国際色豊かなレストランがあると言っている。Dが正解。

A. 彼はいいレストランを経営している。

B. 彼はホテルを知っていると思う。

C. 彼はいいデパートをたくさん知っているようだ。

D. 彼は神戸の国際色豊かなレストランを高く評価している。

ナレーション

Woman: What's there to do in Kobe?

Man:　　Kobe has many great international restaurants.

Question　What does the man mean?

(女)：神戸には何があるんですか。

(男)：神戸には国際色豊かなレストランがたくさんあります。

質問　男性は何と言っていますか。

19. 解答：A

解説 女性は男性に「さあ，どうぞ」と快く車で空港まで乗せてあげると言っている。Aが正解。

A. 彼女は彼を車に乗せてやる。

B. 彼女は彼にお金を貸すだろう。

C. 彼は彼女を助けるだろう。

D. 彼女は私を助けることができない。

ナレーション

Man:　　Could you possibly give me a ride to the airport?

Woman: Hop in!

Question　What does the woman mean?

(男)：空港まで乗せていってもらえませんか。

(女)：どうぞ乗ってください。

質問　女性は何と言っていますか。

20.　解答：D

解説　男性は女性と久しぶりに会った理由を伝えている。D が正解。

A. 彼は退職してパリにいる。

B. 彼はパリにときどき住んでいた。

C. 彼は何度も引っ越したことがある。

D. 彼はパリで仕事をしている。

ナレーション

Woman: Jack, I haven't seen you for so long!

Man:　　I've been working in Paris for ten years.

Question　What does the man mean?

(女)：ジャック，ずいぶん久しぶりね。

(男)：パリで 10 年働いているんだ。

質問　男性は何と言っていますか。

III

まとまりのある内容の英文（300 語前後）を 2 度聴いたあと，
その内容に関する英語の質問を聴いて答えるリスニングテスト。10 問出題。

21.　解答：C

解説　"Once there was a thunderstorm with blinding rain and a tiny wet kitten crying as loudly as it could." から，正解は C。

A. 暑かった。　　B. 曇っていた。

C. 雨が降っていた。　　D. 晴れていた。

22.　解答：B

解説　"Seven-year-old Hiroshi knew the kitten was abandoned." から，正解は B。

A. それにはおそらく家があったのだろう。

B. それは明らかに捨てられていた。

C. それは危険だった。　　D. それはおとなしかった。

23.　解答：A

解説　"He put the kitten inside his jacket" から，正解は A。

A. 彼はそれを上着の中に入れた　　B. 彼はそれを肩の上に置いた。
C. 彼はそれに食べ物をやった。　　D. 彼はそれを手放した。

24. 解答：D

解説 “Hiroshi lived alone with his father who was worried because he was home late in the rising storm.” から，正解は D。

A. 彼は怒っていた。　　B. 彼は幸せだった。
C. 彼は眠かった。　　D. 彼は心配していた。

25. 解答：B

解説 “Take a hot bath,” とヒロシの父親が言っていることから，正解は B。

A. 外に出る　　B. 熱い風呂に入る　　C. 夕食を食べる　　D. 寝る

26. 解答：A

解説 “Hiroshi’s wet clothes on the floor revealed the kitten.” から，正解は A。

A. 子猫　　B. 子犬　　C. コイン　　D. タオル

27. 解答：C

解説 “They called the kitten “Mi-nyan” and decided to keep him.” から，正解は C。

A. 別の飼い主を探すこと　　B. 檻《おり》の中に入れること
C. 飼うこと　　D. 友達に貸す

28. 解答：D

解説 “He was strange in one way: he refused to go outside.” から，正解は D。

A. それはずっと泣いていた。　　B. それは噛《か》んだり引っ掻《か》いたりした。
C. それはずっと外にいた。　　D. それは決して外に出なかった。

29. 解答：D

解説 “One night, Mi-nyan jumped on Hiroshi’s bed and cried, scratched and bit him for the first time. Then he went to his father’s bed and did the same thing." から，正解は D。

A. それは泣いた。　B. それは彼らを引っ掻いた。

C. それは彼らに噛みついた。　D. 上記すべて。

30. 解答：C

解説 "Gas leak!" と父親が言っていることから，正解は C。

A. それはお腹が空いていた。　B. それは外に出たかった。

C. それはガスが漏れているのを感じた。　D. それは寂しかった。

ナレーション

Once there was a thunderstorm with blinding rain and a tiny wet kitten crying as loudly as it could. Seven-year-old Hiroshi knew the kitten was abandoned. He put the kitten inside his jacket and hurried home.

Hiroshi lived alone with his father who was worried because he was home late in the rising storm.

"Take a hot bath," his father said.

Hiroshi's wet clothes on the floor revealed the kitten.

"Mew," it said.

The father took another towel. "We must warm the kitty quickly."

He and his father accepted the kitten easily. They had adopted dogs and cats before and given them to friends. They called the kitten "Mi-nyan" and decided to keep him.

Mi-nyan was a striped cat who neither bit nor scratched. He was strange in one way: he refused to go outside. Hiroshi's father worked from home and could easily see to Mi-nyan when Hiroshi was at school.

One night, Mi-nyan jumped on Hiroshi's bed and cried, scratched and bit him for the first time. Then he went to his father's bed and did the same thing.

"Gas leak!" his father cried. "Open the windows, Hiroshi. I'll try to stop the gas. Call the fire department!"

Afterwards a fireman said, "This is absolutely the smartest cat

I've ever seen."

Questions 21. How was the weather when Hiroshi found the crying kitten?

22. What did Hiroshi assume about the cat?

23. What did Hiroshi do with the kitten?

24. How was his father when Hiroshi came home?

25. What did his father tell Hiroshi to do?

26. What did the father find in Hiroshi's wet clothes?

27. What did Hiroshi and his father decide to do with the kitten?

28. What was particular about the kitten?

29. How did the kitten wake Hiroshi and his father up?

30. Why did the kitten wake them up?

訳例　あるとき，雷雨で一寸先も見えない雨が降り，濡れた小さな子猫が大声で泣いていました。7歳のヒロシは，その子猫が捨てられたとわかっていました。彼は子猫を上着の中に入れて，急いで家に帰りました。

ヒロシは父と二人暮らしで，嵐の中，彼が遅くまで家に帰ってこないので父親は心配していました。

「熱い風呂に入りなさい」と父親は言いました。

床にあったヒロシの濡れた服から子猫が見えました。

「ニャン」と子猫は泣きました。

父親は別のタオルを取りました。「子猫を早く暖めよう」

ヒロシと父親は，子猫をすぐに受け入れました。彼らは以前から犬や猫を飼ったり，友達にあげたりしていました。そして，その子猫を「ミーニャン」と名付け，飼うことにしました。

ミーニャンは，噛んだり，引っ掻いたりしない，縞模様の猫でした。ただ，1点だけ不思議だったのは，外に出るのを嫌がることでした。ヒロシの父親は在宅勤務で，ヒロシが学校に行っている間，ミーニャンの面倒を見ることができました。

ある夜，ミーニャンはヒロシのベッドに飛び乗って泣き，初めて彼を引っ掻いたり，噛みついたりしました。そして，ヒロシの父親のベッドに行き，同じことをしました。

「ガス漏れだ！」と父親が叫びました。「窓を開けてくれ，ヒロシ。私はガスを止める。消防署に電話しろ！」

その後，消防士が「いままで見た中でいちばん賢い猫だ」と言いました。

質問　21. ヒロシが泣いている子猫を見つけたときの天気はどうでした

か。

22. ヒロシはその猫についてどんなことを想定していましたか。
23. ヒロシはその子猫をどうしましたか。
24. ヒロシが家に帰ったとき，彼の父親はどうでしたか。
25. 父親はヒロシに何をするように言いましたか。
26. 父親はヒロシの濡れた服の中から何を見つけましたか。
27. ヒロシと父親は子猫をどうすることにしましたか。
28. 子猫のどこが特別だったのですか。
29. 子猫はどのようにしてヒロシと父親を起こしましたか。
30. 子猫はなぜ2人を起こしたのですか。

IV

会話を2度聴いたあと，
その内容に関する英語の質問を聴いて答えるリスニングテスト。10問出題。

ユキとジョーが話をしています

31. 解答：B

解説 ジョーが“Wow! The patterns are unique, and the colors are vivid!”と言っていることから，正解はB。

A. 面白くなくて，ありふれている
B. 鮮やかで個性的
C. 素敵だが，刺激的でない
D. ジョーは女性の服を理解していない。

32. 解答：A

解説 ユキが“I made the dress myself.”と言っていることから，正解はA。

A. ユキが作った。　B.　ある会社が作った。
C. 彼女の仕立屋が作った。　D.　ジョーが作った。

33. 解答：B

解説 ユキが“I'm learning dressmaking from an African dressmaker.”と言っていることから，正解はB。

A. 彼女の母親　B. 仕立屋さん　C. 誰でもない　D. ジョー

34. 解答：A

解説 ユキが“The material is from a country in Africa.”と言っていることから，正解はA。

A. アフリカ　B. 日本　C. ヨーロッパ　D. オーストラリア

35. 解答：C

解説 ユキが“Her fabrics are also suitable for men.”と言っていることから，正解はC。

A. 決して使えない　B. 多分使える

C. 使える　D. お祭りのときだけ

36. 解答：D

解説 ユキが“And her clothing is good for all seasons in Japan.”と言っていることから，正解はD。

A. 特に春や夏にはとても快適だ。

B. 冬に着るのが1番いい。

C. 秋が1番快適だ。

D. 仕立屋は季節を問わず快適なものを作ってくれる。

37. 解答：B

解説 ユキが“We can all have lunch or dinner. She’s vegetarian. I hope you don’t mind.”と言っていることから，正解はB。

A. 飲みに行く　B. ベジタリアンレストランで食事をする

C. 魚を食べる　D. 肉を食べる

38. 解答：D

解説 ユキが“She makes old clothes look like new.”と言っていることから，正解はD。

A. 彼女はそれらを捨てている。

B. 彼女は貧しい人々にそれらを与える。

C. 彼女はそれらをリサイクルに出す。

D. 彼女は古い服を新しい服に作り変える。

39.　解答：D

解説 国名は述べられていないことから，正解はD。

A. ザンビア　　B. 南アフリカ

C. エチオピア　　D. 述べられていない

40.　解答：C

解説 優れた仕立屋さんについてユキとジョーが話をしていることから，正解はC。

A. 映画スターの服　　B. 古着の処分方法

C. 卓越した仕立屋さん　　D. ベジタリアン料理が体にいい理由

ナレーション

Yuki: How do you like my new dress?

Joe: Wow! The patterns are unique, and the colors are vivid!

Yuki: I made the dress myself. The material is from a country in Africa.

Joe: I didn't know you were a dressmaker.

Yuki: I'm learning dressmaking from an African dressmaker. She's very kind and patient with me.

Joe: Can she make men's clothing?

Yuki: She sure can! Her fabrics are also suitable for men. And her clothing is good for all seasons in Japan.

Joe: I'd like to meet your dressmaker!

Yuki: We can all have lunch or dinner. She's vegetarian. I hope you don't mind.

Joe: Vegetarian is fine with me. I'd really like her to make a shirt for me.

Yuki: She can lay out the patterns before we go out to eat. Her methods for making clothing are guided by feeling and logic.

Joe: Is her clothing expensive?

Yuki: Surprisingly not that expensive. There is one thing she insists on. She doesn't want you to throw her clothing away.

Joe: You mean she recycles it?

Yuki: Better than that. She makes old clothes look like new.

Joe: I really want to meet your friend.

Questions 31. How does Joe regard Yuki's new dress?

32. Who made Yuki's dress?

33. Who is teaching Yuki to make dresses?

34. Where are the dressmaker's fabrics from?

35. Can the fabrics be used for men's clothing too?

36. How comfortable are the dressmaker's clothes?

37. What will they do when Yuki introduces Joe to her dressmaker?

38. What does the dressmaker do with old clothes?

39. Where in Africa is the dressmaker from?

40. What would be the best title for this story?

訳例 ユキ： 新しいドレスはどう？

ジョー：わぁー！ 柄もユニークだし，色も鮮やかだね。

ユキ： この服は自分で作ったの。素材はアフリカの国のものよ。

ジョー：君が服を作れるって知らなかったなぁ。

ユキ： アフリカの仕立屋さんから洋裁を教わっているの。彼女はとても親切で我慢強いのよ。

ジョー：彼女は男性の服も作れるの？

ユキ： 作れるわ。彼女の生地は男性用にも適しているの。それに，彼女の作る服は日本のどの季節でも着られるのよ。

ジョー：仕立屋さんに会ってみたいな。

ユキ： みんなでランチかディナーをしましょう。彼女はベジタリアンなの。かまわないでしょう。

ジョー：ベジタリアンでかまわないよ。ぜひ，僕のシャツを作ってほしいんだ。

ユキ： 食事に行く前に彼女は型紙を（布地に）配置できるわ。彼女の服作りの方法は感覚と理論でやっているの。

ジョー：彼女の作る服は高いの？

ユキ： 意外と高くないのよ。ただ，ひとつだけこだわりがあるわ。彼女の服を捨ててほしくないということなの。

ジョー：リサイクルしているってこと？

ユキ： もっといい方法があるのよ。彼女は古い服を新品同様に仕上げてくれるの。

ジョー：君の友達にぜひ会ってみたいな。

質問 31. ジョーはユキの新しいドレスをどのように思っていますか。

32. ユキのドレスは誰が作りましたか。
33. 誰がユキにドレス作りを教えているのですか。
34. 仕立屋さんの生地はどこのものですか。
35. その生地は紳士服にも使えるのですか。
36. 仕立屋さんの服の着心地はどうですか。
37. ユキがジョーに仕立屋さんを紹介するとき，2人は何をするのですか。
38. 仕立屋さんは古着をどうするのですか。
39. 仕立屋さんはアフリカのどこの国の人ですか。
40. この話の題名に最もふさわしいのはどれですか。

V

英文の下線部の意味を最もよく表す語または語句を4つの選択肢中から1つ選ぶ問題。10問出題。

41. 解答：B

解説 be at each other's throats は「激しく争っている，対立している」の意味なので，B が正解。

訳例 彼らは激しく争っている。

A. 仲のいい友達だ　B. お互いを嫌っている
C. お互いに恋をしている　D. お互いを知らない

42. 解答：A

解説 point of view は「考え方，意見」の意味なので，A が正解。

訳例 彼女は自分の考えを上手に表現しました。

A. 考え　B. 絵　C. プレゼント　D. 挨拶

43. 解答：D

解説 look up to は「尊敬する」の意味なので，D が正解。

訳例 彼は大統領を尊敬しています。

A. 訓練する　B. 真似する　C. 軽蔑する　D. 敬服する

44. 解答：B

解説 make out は「理解する」の意味なので，B が正解。

訳例 この詩の意味がわかりますか。

A. 塗る　B. 理解する　C. 広告する　D. 埋める

45. 解答：C

解説 count on は「頼りにする」の意味なので，C が正解。

訳例 彼女はあなたを頼りにしています。

A. 受け入れる　B. 同情する　C. 頼りにする　D. 一緒に暮らす

46. 解答：A

解説 lose face は「面目を失う，恥をかく」の意味なので，A が正解。

訳例 彼は観客の前で面目を失った。

A. 屈辱を味わった　B. ポイントを獲得した

C. 解答を得た　D. 気分が悪かった

47. 解答：B

解説 cannot help but 動詞原形は「することが避けられない，せずにはいられない」の意味なので，B が正解。

訳例 彼は大声で話さずにはいられません。

A. 喜んでやる　B. ～するしか仕方ない　C. 助けが必要だ　D. 断る

48. 解答：D

解説 lose faith in は「信頼を失う，信用できなくなる」の意味なので，D が正解。

訳例 私はリーダーへの信頼を失いました。

A. 好きだった　B. 嫌いだった　C. 無関心だった　D. 失望した

49. 解答：B

解説 move は「感動させる」，be moved で「感動する」の意味なので，B が正解。

訳例 私は彼女の優しさに感動した。

A. 傷ついた　B. 感動した　C. 嫌になった　D. 退屈した

50. 解答：C

解説 stage by stage は「徐々に，段階を経て」の意味なので，C が正解。

訳例 彼のピアノは徐々に上達している。

A. 速く　B. 完璧に　C. 少しずつ　D. ぜんぜんだめ

VI

300～400語程度のまとまりのある文を国連英検指定テキスト『新 わかりやすい国連の活動と世界』から抜粋し，その内容を把握しているかどうかを問う問題。10題出題。

51. 解答：C

解説 “The establishment of the Peacebuilding Commission (PBC) was proposed during the World Summit of the United Nations” から，C が正解。

訳例　平和構築委員会はどのような組織で設置が提案されましたか。
A. 総会　B. 信託統治理事会
C. 国際連合の世界サミット　D. 経済社会理事会

52. 解答：A

解説 “The United Nations not only helps to end conflicts, but also plays a role in preventing conflict-affected countries (or regions) from relapsing into civil war.” から，A が正解。

訳例　本文によると，国連の役割の 1 つは何ですか。
A. 紛争が内戦に再燃するのを防ぐこと　B. 1 つの強力な国を強化すること
C. 国連の利益を促進すること　D. 女性団体を排除すること

53. 解答：B

解説 “To promote ‘sustaining peace,’ the Commission takes a consistent approach to making suggestions and proposals on comprehensive strategies for the post-conflict process of peacebuilding and restoration from conflict resolution to restoration, and from reintegration to reconstruction.” から，B が正解。

訳例　本文によると，平和構築委員会の仕事について，次のうち正しくないものはどれですか。
A.「平和の維持」を促進する。
B. 平和構築のための 1 つの戦略だけに関する提案や提言をする。
C. 平和構築と復旧という紛争後のプロセスを支援することを目的としている。
D. その戦略は，紛争解決から復旧まで，また社会復帰から復興まで，多岐にわたる。

54. 解答：B

解説 "The Peacebuilding Commission is an intergovernmental advisory body composed of 31 Member States elected from the General Assembly, the Security Council, and the Economic and Social Council." から，B が正解。

訳例 平和構築委員会の 31 の加盟国はどのように決まるのですか。

A. 総会の指名による

B. 総会，安全保障理事会，経済社会理事会による選挙で決定する

C. 信託統治領からの指名による

D. 紛争の影響を受けている国からの選挙による

55. 解答：C

解説 "Within the United Nations Systems, the Peacebuilding Commission is an unprecendented organization in that its mandate includes the authority to provide advice to the Security Council, the General Assembly and the Economic and Social Council on critical issues of peacebuilding." から，C が正解。

訳例 平和構築委員会の特徴は何ですか。

A. 総会，安全保障理事会，経済社会理事会の命令に従わなければならない。

B. 総会，安全保障理事会，経済社会理事会は，平和構築委員会に助言を与える。

C. 平和構築の重要な問題について，総会，安全保障理事会，経済社会理事会に助言を与える権限を有する。

D. 平和構築の重要な問題について，総会，安全保障理事会，経済社会理事会に助言を与えるという任務を回避する。

56. 解答：A

解説 "The United Nations has established the Peacebuilding Architecture, which consists of not only the Peacebuilding Commission, but also the Peacebuilding Support Office (PBSO) and the Peacebuilding Fund (PBF)." から，A が正解。

訳例 平和構築アーキテクチャーを構成する 3 つの機関とは何ですか。

A. 平和構築委員会，平和構築支援室，平和構築基金

B. 総会，国際金融機関，青年組織

C. 信託統治理事会，女性団体，地域団体

D. 総会，安全保障理事会，経済社会理事会

57. 解答：D

解説 “This architecture of three new bodies was added to the United Nations System in 2005-2006 to strengthen efforts to help post-conflict countries to build sustainable peace and prevent relapse into violent conflict.” から，D が正解。

訳例 平和構築アーキテクチャーが国連システムに追加された目的は何ですか。

A. 政治力の集中が紛争に発展しないように強化するため。
B. 平和構築アーキテクチャーのために働く従業員を増やすため。
C. 総会，安全保障理事会，経済社会理事会に助言を与える権限を強化するため。
D. 紛争後の国が持続可能な平和を構築し，暴力的な紛争の再発を防止するための努力を強化するため。

58. 解答：C

解説 “Security Council Resolution 2282 of 2016 reaffirms that the Peacebuilding Commission has a number of important missions, including bringing sustained international attention to sustaining peace as well as serving as a platform to convene all relevant actors within and outside the United Nations,” から，C が正解。

訳例 本文によると，平和構築委員会の使命について，次のうち誤っているものはどれですか。

A. 平和の維持に国際的な関心を持続的に集めること。
B. 国連以外で招集される関係機関には，国際機構，地域機構，準地域的な機構を含む。
C. 国際連合以外のすべての関係機関を招集するためのプラットフォームとして務めること。
D. 国際連合の外で招集される関係機関には，市民社会，女性グループ，青少年団体，そして関連する場合は民間部門と国内人権機関を含む。

59. 解答：D

解説 “The Trusteeship Council deliberated the administration and supervision of the trust territories, including those detached from enemy states as a result of the Second World War.” から，D が正解。

訳例　信託統治理事会は何を審議しましたか。

A. 独立国の管理　　B. 紛争国の監督

C. 紛争後の国の管理と監督　　D. 信託統治地域の管理と監督

60.　解答：D

解説　suspendは「中断する」の意味だから，Dが正解。

訳例　下線部（60）“suspend”は何を意味しますか。

A. 強制された　　B.拡大した　　C. 交換した　　D. 停止した

訳例　平和構築委員会（PBC）は，2005年の世界サミット開催時にその設置が提案された。国連は，紛争を止めるだけでなく，紛争に影響を受けた国（または地域）において内戦が再燃することを防ぐ役割も果たしている。「持続可能な平和」を促進するために，平和構築委員会は，紛争状態の解決から復旧，社会復帰，復興に至るまで，一貫したアプローチに基づき，紛争後の平和構築と復旧のための統合戦略を助言及び提案する。

平和構築委員会は，総会，安全保障理事会，経済社会理事会から選出された31の加盟国によって構成される政府間諮問機関である。国連システムの中で平和構築委員会は，安全保障理事会，総会，経済社会理事会に平和構築の決定的に重要な問題について，助言を与えることを含む，先例のない組織であり権限を持っている。国連は，平和構築委員会に加えて，平和構築支援事務局（PBSO），平和構築基金（PBF）からなる平和構築アーキテクチャーを創設した。国連が持続可能な平和を構築し，暴力的な紛争への再発を予防するための努力を強化するために，この3つの新機関のアーキテクチャーが2005–2006年に加えられた。

また，2016年の安保理決議2282は，平和構築委員会が，「平和の持続」に対して，持続的で国際的な注意をもたらすこと，および加盟国，国の当局，国際連合ミッションおよび国別現地チーム，国際的な，地域的なまた準地域的な機構，国際金融機関，市民社会，女性の集団，青年組織および，関連する場合には，民間部門と国内人権機関からのものを含む，国際連合内外の全ての関連する関係者を招集するプラットフォームとして務めることの重要性を強調している。

なお，平和構築委員会の会合の多くは信託統治理事会の会議室を利用して開催されている。信託統治理事会は，第2次世界大戦の結果として敵国から分離された地域などが独立を達成するまで，信託統治地域の統治および監督について審議した。1994年11月に最後の信託統治地域であるパラオが独立したのちに，信託統治理事会はその作業を停止した。

『新 わかりやすい国連の活動と世界』pp. 57–58

VII 2つの文章に共通して用いられる語を1つ，選択肢の中から選ぶ問題。
10問出題。

61. 解答：B

解説 brand は名詞で「銘柄，ブランド」，動詞で「(人) に〜だという烙印《らくいん》を押す，〜だと決めつける」の意味。正解は B。

訳例 「私はデザインがいいからこのブランドが気に入っています」
「彼にうそつきの烙印を押さないでください」
A. メーカー　C. 器具　D. 顧客

62. 解答：A

解説 comfort は他動詞で「を慰める，元気づける」，名詞で「くつろぎ，安らぎ」の意味。正解は A。

訳例 「私は彼を慰めなければなりません」
「家にいると安らぐ」
B. 座席　C. 泣く　D. 問題

63. 解答：D

解説 excess は名詞で「超過，超過額」，to excess で「過度に」の意味。正解は D。

訳例 「私は超過額 100 ドルを支払いました」
「彼は食べ過ぎました」
A. 努力　B. 興味　C. を超えて

64. 解答：C

解説 flag は動詞で「印をつける」，flag down で「(乗物，運転手) に合図をして止める」，名詞で「旗」の意味。正解は C。

訳例 「彼女はタクシーを呼び止めるでしょう」
「私は彼らの旗が船の上に (掲げられているのが) 見えました」
A. 船長　B. 捕まえる　D. 発見する

65. 解答：A

解説 lean は動詞で「傾く」，lean on で「(人) に頼る」，形容詞で「ほっそりした」の意味。正解は A。

訳例 「あなたは彼に頼ることができます」

「彼女はとてもほっそりしています」
B. 跳ぶ　C. 安定した　D. お願いする

66. 解答：D

解説 mentionは動詞で「に言及する」，Don't mention it. で「(感謝・お詫びに対して) どういたしまして」，名詞で「名を挙げること」の意味。正解はD。

訳例 「どういたしまして」
「彼は特筆に価します」
A. 罰する　B. 港　C. 謎

67. 解答：B

解説 pressureは名詞で「圧力，(精神的な) 重圧，ストレス」，pressure cookerで「圧力鍋」の意味。正解はB。

訳例 「私はこの圧力鍋が気に入っています」
「彼はストレスをたくさん受けています」
A. スズ　C. 損傷　D. 引っ張る

68. 解答：A

解説 nativeは名詞で「(ある土地の) 住民」，形容詞で「原産の，固有の」の意味。正解はA。

訳例 「彼女はフランス語を母語のように話します」
「この木はオーストラリアが原産です」
B. 国家　C. 市民　D. 塔

69. 解答：B

解説 phaseは名詞で「段階，側面」，動詞で「段階的に実行する」，phase outで「を段階的に廃止する」の意味。正解はB。

訳例 「その少年は人生の一段階を経験しています」
「私たちは規則を段階的に廃止します」
A. 危機　C. 変化　D. 減少

70. 解答：C

解説 sortは動詞で「分類する」，sort outで「整理する」，名詞で「〜な人」a

good sort で「感じのよい（信頼できる）人」の意味。正解は C。

訳例　「私たちは服を整理しなければなりません」
「彼はいい人です」
A. と結論を下す　B. 緊張　D. 打撃

Ⅷ　４つの文章の中で，文法的に用法が間違っているものを見つける問題。
10 問出題。

71.　解答：C

was logged at → was logged in

「彼の旅の情報はコンピューターに記録された」

解説　log の用法を問う問題。A の log は名詞で「丸太」，B の log in は「(コンピューター）にログインする」，D の sleep like a log は「ぐっすり眠る」の意味。C の log は他動詞で「記録する」，log in the computer で「コンピューターに記録する」の意味なので，was logged at ではなく was logged in が正しい。C が正解。

訳例　A. 彼女は丸太を使って筏《いかだ》を作っています。
B. あなたはコンピューターにログインする必要があります。
D. 彼は昨夜ぐっすり眠りました。

72.　解答：C

a fun → fun

「楽しんでください」

解説　fun の用法を問う問題。A の fun は名詞で「楽しみ」，B の make fun of は「をからかう，笑い者にする」，D の fun は形容詞で「楽しい」，a fun time は「楽しい時間」の意味。C の fun は不可算名詞なので，a fun ではなく fun が正しい。C が正解。

訳例　A. なんと楽しいことでしょう。
B. 彼女は人をからかうのが好きではありません。
D. 彼は動物園で楽しい時間を過ごしました。

73.　解答：A

rains or shines → rain or shine

「どんなことがあっても私はあなたのウェディングパーティーに行きます」

解説　rain の用法を問う問題。B の rain は動詞で「雨が降る」，C の be rained

out は「(雨) で中止 (延期) になる」，D の a rain check は「(今回はだめだが) 次の機会には受け入れる」の意味。A は rain or shine で「晴雨にかかわらず，どんなことがあっても」の意味なので，rains or shines ではなく rain or shine が正しい。A が正解。

訳例 B. 冬はよく雨が降ります。
C. ピクニックは雨で中止になった。
D. ディナーパーティーは次の機会にお願いします。

74. 解答：A

good to → good for

「列車の乗車券は 1 日有効です」

解説 good の用法を問う問題。B の good は「十分な」good chance で「十分ありうる可能性」，C の for good は「ずっと，永久に」，D の for your own good「自分のためを思って」の意味。A は「有効期間」の意味なので，good to ではなく good for が正しい。A が正解。

訳例 B. そのテニスプレーヤーは試合に勝つチャンスが十分あります。
C. 彼女は故郷でずっと暮らしたいと思っています。
D. 自分のために行動してください。

75. 解答：B

teach → show (or tell)

「駅への行き方を教えてください」

解説 teach の用法を問う問題。A の teach は「教える」，C は「(仕方) を教える」，D は「(教訓など) を与える，思い知らせる」の意味。B は「駅への行き方を教える」の意味なので，teach ではなく show または tell が正しい。B が正解。

訳例 A. 彼女は短大で教鞭《きょうべん》をとっています。
C. 彼は運転の仕方を私に教えてくれました。
D. 彼女は彼に忘れられない教訓を与えました。

76. 解答：C

at the way → in the way

「道に故障したトラックがありました」

解説 way の用法を問う問題。A の in more ways than one は「いろいろな

意味で」，B の on one's way は「途中で」，D の all the way は「はるばる，わざわざ」の意味。C は「道路で」の意味なので，at the way ではなく in the way が正しい。C が正解。

訳例　A. 彼女はいろいろな意味で才能がある。
B. 彼は通学途中に旧友に会った。
D. 彼女は姉に会いにはるばるニューヨークまで行った。

77.　解答：D

equally match → equally matched

「そのテニスプレーヤーは互角です」

解説　match の用法を問う問題。A の a love match は「相思相愛」，B の match は「と調和する，似合う」，C の the tennis match は「テニスの試合」の意味。D は equally matched で「対等である，互角である」の意味なので，equally match ではなく equally matched が正しい。D が正解。

訳例　A. 2 人は相思相愛です。
B. 真珠のネックレスは彼女のドレスに合っています。
C. 彼女は昨夜のテニスの試合で勝ちました。

78.　解答：B

home → the home

「ニューオリンズはジャズの本場です」

解説　home の用法を問う問題。A の a nursing home は「老人ホーム」，C の home economics は「家政学」，D の at home は「在宅して」の意味。B は the home で「発祥地，本場」の意味なので，home ではなく the home が正しい。B が正解。

訳例　A. 彼は老人ホームに住んでいます。
C. 彼女は家政学に興味があります。
D. 荷物が届けられたとき，彼は家にいました。

79.　解答：D

more happy → the happier

「休暇のことを考えれば考えるほど，私はうれしくなりました」

解説　比較級の用法を問う問題。A の higher and higher は「ますます上がって」，B の more A than B は「B よりむしろ A（という方が適切)」，C

の not ... any more は「もはや…しない」の意味。D は the 比較級，the 比較級の構文で，the more ...，the more ... で「…が多くなればなるほど…が多くなる」の意味なので，more happy ではなく the happier が正しい。D が正解。

訳例　A. 価格がどんどん上がっています。
B. 彼女は先生というより芸術家です。
C. 私はもう彼に会うことはないでしょう。

80.　解答：D

show on → show up

「私は彼を待ちましたが，彼は現われませんでした」

解説　show の用法を問う問題。A の show O around は「(人を) 案内して回る」，B の show off は「ひけらかす」，C の It goes to show は「ということを証明している」の意味。D は show up で「現れる」の意味なので，show on ではなく show up が正しい。D が正解。

訳例　A. 彼女は私に彼女の家の案内をしてくれました。
B. 彼は自分の財産を見せびらかすのが好きではありません。
C. 食べ物は健康のために大切だということははっきりしています。

IX

300 語前後のまとまりのある文を読み，読解力を試す問題。
空所補充，語句の並べ替え，語彙力，行間を読む力を問う問題を 10 問出題。

81.　解答：D

解説　“Russia’s shelling of Chernobyl’s nuclear power plant in Ukraine sparked a fire at one of its six reactors, stirring fears of a 1986-like meltdown.” から，D が正解。

訳例　チェルノービリ原発での「かき立てられる恐怖」とは何ですか。
A. ロシアの爆撃　　B. 原子炉の 1 基での火災
C. メルトダウンの恐れ　　D. 上記のすべて

82.　解答：C

解説　“The International Atomic Energy Agency (IAEA) warned that war in and around such nuclear facilities presents extreme risks.” から，C が正解。

訳例　原子力発電所に「極度のリスクをもたらす」ものは何ですか。

A. 古すぎること　B. 予備部品がないこと
C. 原子力発電所付近での戦争　D. 最新技術

83. 解答：B

解説 "A failure of those systems could lead to a meltdown disaster similar to that of Japan's Fukushima plant." から，B が正解。

訳例 チェルノービリの原子炉がメルトダウンしたら，どうなりますか。
A. 全く何も起こらない。
B. 福島原子力発電所のような惨事が起こる。
C. 小さな問題しか起きない。
D. チェルノービリ原子力発電所が再び稼働する。

84. 解答：C

解説 "Ukrainian President, Volodymyr Zelenskyy, declared in the middle of the night, 'If there is an explosion, that's the end of everyone. The end of Europe.'" から，C が正解。

訳例 ウクライナのヴォロディミル・ゼレンスキー大統領は，チェルノービリについて何と言いましたか。
A.「眠りにつくがいい。何も心配することはない。」
B.「プーチンに話す。彼は私たちを助けてくれるだろう。」
C.「もし爆発が起きたら，みんな終わりだ。ヨーロッパの終わりだ。」
D.「ロシア軍を破壊するだろう。戦争はなくなる。」

85. 解答：A

解説 "He called for an end to fighting near the plant." から，A が正解。

訳例 ゼレンスキーは何を呼びかけましたか。
A. チェルノービリ原子力発電所周辺での戦闘の停止
B. ウクライナ人にロシア人を攻撃するよう奨励すること
C. キーウからすぐに脱出すること
D. チェルノービリの心配をしないようにすること

86. 解答：C

解説 "One expert said that the loss of off-site electrical power could force the plant to rely on emergency diesel generators, which are highly unreliable and could fail or run out of fuel," から，C が正解。

訳例　現在チェルノービリ原子力発電所で最悪の問題になっていることは何ですか。
A. チェルノービリ原子炉内での核爆発
B. チェルノービリ原子力発電所から撤退するロシア人
C. 信頼性の低いディーゼル発電機の故障や燃料切れの可能性
D. ウクライナ人がロシアを攻撃すること

87.　解答：C

解説　"Ukraine is heavily reliant on nuclear energy, with 15 reactors at four stations that provide about half the country's electricity." から，Cが正解。

訳例　ウクライナはどのようなエネルギー問題を抱えていますか。
A. 原子力発電所が1つしかない。
B. 原子力発電所が1つもない。
C. 原子力発電に大きく依存している。
D. 太陽光発電に大きく依存している。

88.　解答：D

解説　"In an appeal to the IAEA for help, Ukrainian officials said that the Chernobyl staff have been held by the Russian military without rotation and are exhausted. Ukraine appealed to Russia to let the regular Ukrainian Chernobyl staff 'do their job safely and effectively.'" から，Dが正解。

訳例　IAEAへの協力の要請はどのような内容ですか。
A. チェルノービリのスタッフがロシア軍に拘束されている。
B. チェルノービリのスタッフを交替させず，彼らは疲弊している。
C. ロシア軍はチェルノービリのスタッフを安全かつ効果的に働かせるべきである。
D. 上記のすべて。

89.　解答：B

解説　"During warfare, the danger of a meltdown becomes more likely." から，Bが正解。

訳例　チェルノービリ原子力発電所でメルトダウンが起こる危険性の原因は何ですか。
A. 平和　B. 戦争　C. 悪天候　D. 上記のすべて

90. 解答：B

解説 記事全体の内容によると，チェルノービリや周辺での戦争とその危険について述べられているから，B が正解。

訳例 この記事に最もふさわしいタイトルは何ですか。

A. チェルノービリの問題は軽微である

B. チェルノービリへの戦争と危険

C. 恐ろしい爆発がチェルノービリを揺るがす

D. チェルノービリ観光ツアー

訳例 ウクライナのチェルノービリ原子力発電所へのロシアの爆撃は，その 6 つの原子炉の 1 基で火災を引き起こし，1986 年のようなメルトダウンの恐怖をかき立てた。ウクライナの作業員が火を消した。しかし，原子炉コンパートメントに損傷を受けた。国際原子力機関（IAEA）は，このような原子力施設内や周辺での戦争は非常に危険であると警告している。

ウクライナの国家原子力規制当局は，もし戦闘によって原子力発電所への電力供給が中断されれば，稼働中の冷却システムに緊急電力を供給するために信頼性の低いディーゼル発電機を使用せざるを得なくなるだろうと警告した。それらのシステムの故障は，日本の福島原子力発電所のようなメルトダウンの惨事をもたらすかもしれない。

ウクライナ大統領ヴォロディミル・ゼレンスキーは「もし爆発が起これば，それは皆の終わりです。ヨーロッパの終わりです」と，真夜中に宣言した。彼は原子力発電所付近での戦闘を終わらせるよう呼びかけた。

被害を受けた原子炉は停止していたが，高濃度の放射性核燃料は残っている。他の 6 つの原子炉のうち 4 基は現在停止中で，稼働しているのは 1 基だけである。

おそらく最大の懸念は，原子力発電所の電力供給であろう。ある専門家によると，敷地外の電力が失われた場合，原子力発電所は非常用ディーゼル発電機に頼らざるを得なくなるが，この発電機は信頼性が非常に低く，故障や燃料切れで停電となり，使用済み燃料プールを冷却するために必要な水の循環が停止する可能性があるとのことである。

ウクライナは原子力エネルギーに大きく依存しており，4 つの発電所に 15 基の原子炉があり，国の電力の約半分をまかなっている。

ウクライナ当局は，IAEA に助けを求める嘆願の中で，チェルノービリのスタッフはロシア軍によって拘束されており，交替なしで，疲労困憊《こんぱい》していると述べた。ウクライナはロシアに，正規のウクライナ人チェルノービリ・スタッフに「安全かつ効果的に仕事をさせる」よう訴えた。

戦時期には，メルトダウンの危険がより起こりやすい。

X まとまりのある会話文を読み，会話が行われている状況におけるイディオム，語彙力，コミュニケーションの力を試す問題。10 問出題。

91. 解答：D

解説 会話全体を通して理由が述べられていないことから，D が正解。

訳例 ジーナとジローはなぜこんなに会いたがっているのでしょうか。
A. 彼らはボーイフレンドとガールフレンドです。 B. 彼らは兄と妹です。
C. 彼らは友達ではありません。 D. 述べられていません。

92. 解答：D

解説 "I have sequestered myself — but not only because of the pandemic. My back has been in terrible shape for over two weeks." とジローが述べていることから，D が正解。

訳例 なぜジローは家にいたのですか。
A. パンデミック（感染症の世界的大流行）だけの理由でした。
B. 彼は長いレポートを書くのにとても忙しかったからでした。
C. 腰痛だけが理由でした。
D. パンデミックと腰痛のせいでした。

93. 解答：A

解説 "I'll take you to the hospital right away." とジーナが述べていることから，A が正解。

訳例 ジーナはまずどこにジローを連れていくのでしょうか。
A. お医者さんへ行きます。 B. 彼女の家に夕食を食べに行きます。
C. レストランへ行きます。 D. 買い物に行きます。

94. 解答：B

解説 "By the way, you look thinner." とジーナが述べていることから，B が正解。

訳例 ジーナはジローのどんなところに気づいていますか。
A. 彼の声が変わった。 B. 彼は体重が減った。
C. 彼はめまいがする。 D. 彼は眼鏡をかけている。

95. 解答：D

解説 "I have not eaten fast food for two weeks." とジローが述べているこ

とから，D が正解。

訳例　ジローが２週間，食べていないものは何ですか。

A. シチュー　B. 寿司　C. オーガニックフード　D. ファーストフード

96. 解答：B

解説　“Now I can cook pretty well for myself.” とジローが述べていることから，B が正解。

訳例　ジローは料理が上手ですか。

A. 彼は有名な料理人です。　B. 彼は料理が下手ではありません。
C. 述べられていません。　D. 彼はどうしようもないほど料理が下手です。

97. 解答：A

解説　“during my sequestration I learned how to cook through the Internet.” とジローが述べていることから，A が正解。

訳例　ジローが隔離中に発見したことは何ですか。

A. 料理　B. 薬　C. サイクリング　D. 体重の増やし方

98. 解答：C

解説　“I found an Internet site that delivers packages of organic eggs, fruits, vegetables, and meat.” とジローが述べていることから，C が正解。

訳例　ジローは隔離している間，どのように食料品の買い物をしましたか。

A. スーパーマーケットに行きました。
B. ファーストフードを注文しました。
C. インターネットで買い物をしました。
D. 近所の店で食品を買いました。

99. 解答：C

解説　“After we see your doctor, I’ll take you home in my car. Then I’ll do some shopping for you. There are other things you need for your apartment.” とジーナが述べていることから，C が正解。

訳例　医師の診察が終わったら，ジローとジーナは何をするのですか。

A. ジローはジーナと一緒に買い物に行くでしょう。
B. 彼らはタクシーでスーパーマーケットに行きます。

C. ジーナはジローを家に連れて行き，それから買い物に行きます。
D. 彼らはファーストフードを食べに行くでしょう。

100. 解答：B

解説 会話全体を通してジーナが腰痛に悩むジローを病院に連れて行き，ジローのために買い物をするという内容から，B が正解。

訳例 この会話のタイトルとして最も適切なものは何ですか。
A. ファーストフードを食べる　　B. ジーナ，救助に向かう！
C. パンデミック時の楽しみ　　D. ジーナとクッキング

訳例 ジーナ：こんにちは，ジロー。会えてうれしいわ。会いたかったわ。お元気かしら。
ジロー：僕はほとんどアパートから出てないんだ。本当に会いたかったよ。
ジーナ：何をしてたの？
ジーナ：僕は自主隔離をしてたんだ。でもパンデミックのためだけではなくて，腰が 2 週間以上悪かったんだよ。かかりつけの病院の医者に行かなければならないけど，あまりに痛くて。それにバスは混んでいるし新型コロナ感染の危険もあるし。
ジーナ：私はいま，車があるからすぐに病院に連れて行ってあげるわ。
ジロー：ありがとう。主治医に電話して，診てもらえるかどうか聞いてみよう。［電話する］腰が悪いのですが，診てもらえますか。診ていただけるのですね。良かったです。ありがとうございます，先生。
ジーナ：それは良かったわ。歩けるかしら。私の車は遠くないわよ。
ジロー：できるよ。昔，ハイキングに行ったときに使っていた杖があるんだ。
ジーナ：ところで，あなたは細くなったみたい。どうやって痩せたの。
ジロー：2 週間，ファーストフードを食べなかったんだ。たぶん，それで痩せたんだと思う。
ジーナ：自炊をしたの？
ジロー：料理は苦手だったんだけど，隔離している間にインターネットで料理の仕方を覚えたんだ。今は結構自炊ができるようになったよ。
ジーナ：それはすごいね。
ジロー：それだけじゃなくて，オーガニックフードに興味が出てきて，料理も上手にできるようになったんだ。オーガニックの卵や果物，野菜，肉などを宅配してくれるウェブサイトも見つけたんだよ。
ジーナ：腰痛持ちのあなたには，特に便利なサービスね。
ジロー：そのとおり。それに，有機食品は味もいいし，健康にもいいんだ。
ジーナ：お医者さんに診てもらったら，私の車で家まで送るわ。それから，あなたのために買い物をするわ。他にもアパートに必要なものがあるでしょうから。

ジロー：感謝してもしきれないよ。

2022年C級第1回試験　正解一覧

Ⅰ

1. C　2. A　3. C　4. B　5. A　6. D　7. B　8. C　9. D　10. B

Ⅱ

11. D　12. B　13. A　14. C　15. C　16. D　17. B　18. D　19. A　20. D

Ⅲ

21. C　22. B　23. A　24. D　25. B　26. A　27. C　28. D　29. D　30. C

Ⅳ

31. B　32. A　33. B　34. A　35. C　36. D　37. B　38. D　39. D　40. C

Ⅴ

41. B　42. A　43. D　44. B　45. C　46. A　47. B　48. D　49. B　50. C

Ⅵ

51. C　52. A　53. B　54. B　55. C　56. A　57. D　58. C　59. D　60. D

Ⅶ

61. B　62. A　63. D　64. C　65. A　66. D　67. B　68. A　69. B　70. C

Ⅷ

71. C　72. C　73. A　74. A　75. B　76. C　77. D　78. B　79. D　80. D

Ⅸ

81. D　82. C　83. B　84. C　85. A　86. C　87. C　88. D　89. B　90. B

Ⅹ

91. D　92. D　93. A　94. B　95. D　96. B　97. A　98. C　99. C　100. B

2022年
第2回試験
問題

C級試験問題用紙

C級

外務省後援

２０２２年度第２回国際連合公用語

英語検定試験（100分）

受験上の注意

1．問題用紙は試験開始の合図があるまで開いてはいけません。その間に、この**受験上の注意を熟読しておいてください**。

2．**受験番号と氏名を解答用紙**（マークシート）に記入してください。

3．解答用紙の配布は１人１部のみです。複数の配布は致しません。

4．試験開始前は、答案への解答記入は禁止です。

5．マークシートの記入は、必ずＨＢ以上の濃い鉛筆を使って該当箇所を黒く塗りつぶしてください。書き間違いの場合は「アト」が残らないように消してください。マークシートは絶対に折ったり曲げたりしないでください。

6．受験級、受験地区、会場番号、受験番号のマークシートへの記入は監督者の指示に従い、間違いなく記入してください。**（裏表紙の「マークシート記入例」参照）**

7．試験問題についての質問は、印刷が不鮮明な場合を除き、一切受けつけません。

8．中途退室の際は、マークシートを監督者に渡し、他の受験者の迷惑にならないように静かに退室してください。中途退室後の再入室はできません。

9．試験中は他の受験者の妨げとなる行動は慎んでください。また携帯電話等の電源はお切りください。

10．マークシートは監督者に提出し、問題用紙はご自由にお持ち帰りください。

＊試験問題の複製や転載、インターネットへのアップロード等、いかなる媒体への転用を禁止します。

リスニングテストについて

1．リスニングテストは試験開始後、合図があってから実施されます。（40問あります）

2．リスニングテストが始まる前にリスニング問題の指示と内容を読んで、どういう形式のテストなのか、概要をつかんでおいてください。

3．テスト中の発言は、放送機器の具合が悪く放送された英語の聴き取りができない場合を除いて、しないようにしてください。

試験結果について

1．試験の結果は2022年11月24日㈭頃に通知します。

2．その間に住所変更をされた方は、郵便局へ住所変更の届け出を忘れずに行ってください。

3．発表前の試験結果のお問合せには応じられません。

公益財団法人 日本国際連合協会
http://www.unaj.or.jp/

I. これから短い英文を10言います。英文は2回言います。よく聞いて、会話が成り立つように最も適切なものをA、B、C、Dの中から1つ選びなさい。途中でメモを取ってもかまいません。

1. A. I'll see him tomorrow.
B. He's not sure.
C. I'll mail it today.
D. I went to the post office yesterday.

2. A. How many people are attending?
B. I'm late for the meeting.
C. The room is empty.
D. She didn't attend the meeting.

3. A. I feel happy.
B. Don't you want to sing?
C. Do you have hobbies?
D. Reading is my favorite thing.

4. A. Do you like to run?
B. Whenever I have time.
C. I need a change.
D. I jogged last week.

5. A. The road was crowded.
B. I took a taxi.
C. Nobody took the bus.
D. The driver took a shortcut.

6. A. I'll see you at the lobby.
B. I'll bring a lot of friends.
C. At eight tonight.
D. At seven last night.

7. A. I listen to music.
B. I check a dictionary.
C. I go out with my friends.
D. I cook with my family.

8. A. I'm exhausted.
B. I'm starved.
C. What is the test about?
D. Why are you working hard?

9. A. It's been so windy.
B. I got lost.
C. The museum admission fee was expensive.
D. I've heard of his reputation.

10. A. I have an extra one for you.
B. Good for you.
C. Okay, let's go for dinner.
D. The store is far away.

II. これから短い会話を10言います。会話は２回繰り返します。そのあと、会話の内容について10の質問をします。質問も２回繰り返します。よく聞いて、それぞれの質問の答えとして最も適切なものをA、B、C、Dの中から１つ選びなさい。途中でメモを取ってもかまいません。

11. A. The man knows how to fix fountain pens.
B. The man knows a person who can fix the pen.
C. The pen is excellent and should work now.
D. The pen is broken and will never work again.

12. A. She isn't excited.
B. She does not know what to do.
C. She is already working in Japan.
D. She can't wait to get to work in Japan.

13. A. Her car needs more repairs.
B. She'll pick up the car immediately.
C. She'll sell her car.
D. Her car is expensive.

14. A. They are in the wrong jobs.
B. Men's and women's work must be different.
C. You can take any kind of job you want.
D. The woman wants to be a dress designer.

15. A. The woman should seek legal action.
B. The woman needs to buy lunch for the manager.
C. The woman should settle the issue in private.
D. The woman should apologize to the manager.

16. A. He can take or leave the booster shots.
B. She thinks it is essential to have the shots.
C. Her view is that booster shots are dangerous.
D. They agree to put off having booster shots.

17. A. He'll avoid European countries that are hot in summer.
B. He'll only visit Iceland, which has cool summers.
C. He'll visit hot European countries, and then Iceland.
D. It is impossible to say either way.

18. A. She got the painting from the painter.
B. She bought the painting.
C. She found the painting in her garage.
D. She stole the painting.

19. A. He doesn't want to.
B. He is sick.
C. He is busy right now.
D. He'll be happy to help her.

20. A. She is out of coffee.
B. She has only a little coffee left.
C. He can have as much coffee as he wishes.
D. He must pay for the coffee.

III. これから英文を２回繰り返します。そのあと、内容について10の質問をします。質問も２回繰り返します。よく聞いて、それぞれの質問の答えとして最も適切なものをA、B、C、Dの中から1つ選びなさい。途中でメモを取ってもかまいません。

21. A. In the city.
B. In a small village.
C. In a trailer park.
D. In an apartment complex.

22. A. She got lost.
B. She could not find her animals.
C. She could not reach her husband by cellphone.
D. He was angry with her.

23. A. They found her husband.
B. They didn't find her husband.
C. Her husband Jack called the Highway Patrol.
D. The Highway Patrol took the dog and cat.

24. A. Hunt for Jack with the dog and cat.
B. Look for Jack alone.
C. Make the dog and cat leave the house.
D. Give the dog and cat to the Highway Patrol.

25. A. They stayed home.
B. Jean drove away, leaving them outside.
C. They avoided the car.
D. They showed they wanted to be with Jean in the car.

26. A. "Don't fight!" she shouted.
B. "Don't be bothered by me," she said,
C. She told them to be quiet in the back seat.
D. She told them to sit in the front seat.

27. A. She had no idea of what she was doing.
B. She wanted to stay home.
C. She considered going to the hardware store.
D. She would drive to the Highway Patrol.

28. A. They barked and yowled though Jean told them to stop.
B. They alerted Jean of the Highway Patrol.
C. They started to fight.
D. When Jean opened the door, they run away from her.

29. A. The Highway Patrol saved Jack.
B. The dog and cat made her remember a shortcut to the hardware store.
C. A familiar voice called out to Jean.
D. Both B and C are correct.

30. A. Jack had run out of gas.
B. The car had run off the road and was damaged.
C. Jack had lost his way.
D. The Highway Patrol had arrested Jack.

Ⅳ. これから会話を２回繰り返します。そのあと、内容について10の質問をします。質問も２回繰り返します。よく聞いて、それぞれの質問の答えとして最も適切なものをA、B、C、Dの中から１つ選びなさい。途中でメモを取ってもかまいません。

31. A. Her favorite bookstore closed.
B. She lost all her books.
C. She is lonely.
D. She is hungry.

32. A. Groceries.
B. A coffeeshop and poetry readings.
C. Electronic goods.
D. Computers.

33. A. Coffee and cakes.
B. Live poetry readings.
C. Shaking hands with famous poets.
D. Saving time in searching for books.

34. A. Some great books.
B. Pencils and erasers.
C. Electronic books.
D. Flowers.

35. A. They look nice in your house.
B. They don't take up space.
C. They are very easy on your eyes.
D. They look expensive.

36. A. It is possible to publish your own book electronically.
B. Writers have to use much paper.
C. Internet writers always become rich.
D. It is almost impossible to publish electronically.

37. A. Nothing would ever happen.
B. All our electronic information could be destroyed.
C. Only electronic books would disappear.
D. Hard copy books would disappear.

38. A. Walking.
B. Baking.
C. Photography.
D. Music.

39. A. The local used bookstore.
B. The Internet bookstore.
C. Her favorite restaurant.
D. Rock music.

40. A. Getting Rich Through the Internet
B. The Traditional Bookstore vs the Internet Bookstore
C. How to Run a Coffeeshop in a Bookstore
D. How to Bake Homemade Cookies

V．次の英文の下線部の意味を最もよく表す語または語句をA、B、C、Dの中から１つ選びなさい。

41. He lost his shirt in buying stocks.

A. became amazing rich　　B. misplaced his clothing
C. became very poor　　D. quit working for the laundry

42. You're more than welcome.

A. extremely welcomed　　B. not welcomed
C. incredibly tired　　D. arriving safely

43. She is the class's role model.

A. fashion designer　　B. teacher
C. artist　　D. honor student

44. I was embarrassed to death.

A. hospitalized from shock　　B. terribly ashamed
C. nearly murdered　　D. laughing at you all the time

45. I'm beside myself to be back in Dublin.

A. horrified　　B. very happy
C. bewildered　　D. disinterested

46. The ocean is as smooth as glass today.

A. rough　　B. very calm
C. very clean　　D. dangerous

47. She has been having writer's block recently.

A. good luck　　B. much publicity
C. trouble writing　　D. enjoying writing

48. They developed their friendship in an instant.

A. immediately　　B. gradually
C. distantly　　D. shortly

49. That song is so old-fashioned.

A. silly　　B. intelligent
C. famous　　D. outdated

50. He was strong in those days.

A. nowadays　　B. these days

C. yesterday　　D. in the old days

Ⅵ. 次の英文を読み、設問の答えとして最も適切なものをA、B、C、Dの中から1つ選びなさい。

The Economic and Social Council (ECOSOC), which operates under the authority of the General Assembly, coordinates the economic and social work of the United Nations and its specialized agencies. The Economic and Social Council makes recommendations and initiates activities relating to international cooperation for development, world trade, industrialization, natural resources, human rights, the status of women, population, social welfare, education, health and related matters, science and technology, prevention of crime, drug abuse control, and many other economic and social questions.

The Economic and Social Council has 54 members who serve for three years, 18 being elected each year for a three-year term to replace 18 members whose three-year terms have *expired.

Voting in the Economic and Social Council is by simple majority; each member has one vote.

The Charter of the United Nations *empowers the Economic and Social Council: to study and recommend international action on economic, social, cultural, educational, health and related questions; to promote respect for human rights and fundamental freedoms; to call international conferences and prepare **(58)** draft conventions for submission to the General Assembly on matters within its *competence; to negotiate agreements with the specialized agencies, defining their relationship with the United Nations, and to coordinate their activities; to perform services, **(59)** approved by the General Assembly, for Member States and, upon request, specialized agencies; and to consult with *nongovernmental organizations concerned with matters with which the Council deals.

The Economic and Social Council generally holds one *substantive session each year. This annual session used to *alternate between New York and Geneva, but now is held only in New York every year, with the exception of the *Humanitarian Affairs Segment.

The *year-round work of the Economic and Social Council is carried out in **(60)** bodies such as regional commissions and functional commissions. Specialized agencies and related organizations also report annually to the Council.

注）*expired　有効期限が切れる　　*empowers　権限を与える

*competence　法的権限

*nongovernmental organizations　非政府組織、民間公益団体
*substantive session　通常会期　*alternate　交互にする
*Humanitarian Affairs Segment　人道支援部門　*year-round　年間を通じて

51.　Under what authority does the Economic and Social Council operate?

A.　Specialized agencies.
B.　Member States.
C.　Nongovernmental organizations.
D.　The General Assembly.

52.　What does the Economic and Social Council do in relation to international cooperation for development?

A.　It holds sessions.
B.　It keeps reports.
C.　It makes recommendations and initiates activities.
D.　It forms commissions.

53.　How many years do the Economic and Social Council members serve?

A.　For two years.
B.　For three years.
C.　For four years.
D.　For five years.

54.　How does the Economic and Social Council vote?

A.　By simple majority.
B.　By lottery.
C.　By favoritism.
D.　By hierarchy.

55.　What empowers the Economic and Social Council to promote respect for human rights and fundamental freedoms?

A.　The Ministry of Science and Technology.
B.　The Charter of the United Nations.
C.　The General Assembly.
D.　Specialized agencies.

56. Where did the Economic and Social Council used to hold its annual sessions?

A. Tokyo and London.

B. San Francisco and Paris.

C. New York and Geneva.

D. Chicago and Vienna.

57. What do specialized agencies and related organizations annually do in relation with the Economic and Social Council?

A. They give suggestions to solve problems.

B. They suggest session sites.

C. They submit their meeting proposals.

D. They submit their reports.

58. What does the underlined part (58) draft mean?

A. work-in-progress

B. finished composition

C. diary

D. dialogue

59. What does the underlined part (59) approved mean?

A. admired

B. questioned

C. admitted

D. neglected

60. What does the underlined part (60) bodies mean?

A. legs

B. clothes

C. countries

D. organizations

Ⅶ. 次の各組の文の空所には同じ語が入ります。最も適切なものをA、B、C、Dの中から1つ選びなさい。

61. She is a ________ student. That blow is going to ________.

A. bright　B. well　C. smart　D. tasty

62. The ________ Mr. Smith will be honored. I'll be home ________ .

A. now　B. soon　C. yearly　D. late

63. **She likes to _________ the violin. He saw a great _________ yesterday.**

A. play B. orders C. games D. cats

64. **He must avoid _________ . She is in good _________ .**

A. spirits B. alcohol C. fats D. laughter

65. **She bought a _________. _________ out for other cars.**

A. radio B. watch C. dress D. boat

66. **What are you _________ at? I love _________ my car.**

A. looking B. driving C. washing D. crashing

67. **What is the longest _________ you've ever made? I might _________ over your junk on the floor.**

A. dinner B. whistle C. dog D. trip

68. **She is _________ much money this year. His racing car is _________ on the other racing car.**

A. making B. losing C. falling D. gaining

69. **He _________ his wallet. They will _________ a new political party.**

A. fly B. found C. drive D. kiss

70. **The road is _________ here. I finished a _________ draft of my book.**

A. bumpy B. water C. rough D. baby

Ⅷ. 次のA、B、C、Dからなる各組の英文には下線部に誤りを含むものが1つあります。その文を選びなさい。

71. A. Believe it of not, he is a millionaire.

B. Do you believe in God?

C. I don't like to make believe that I'm somebody.

D. I believe her to have been a lawyer.

72. A. The teacher is in favor with the students.

B. The singer has come back in favor among young people.

C. Will you do me a favor?

D. I have a favor to ask for you.

73. A. There was a heel of bread left on the table.
B. He took to his heel when he saw the police officer.
C. She doesn't like to wear shoes with high heels.
D. His dog comes to heel.

74. A. He is in the height of his powers.
B. The plane gained height slowly.
C. She is five feet in heights.
D. He is afraid of heights.

75. A. He mistook me for my friend.
B. I left my cellphone at home as mistake.
C. He made a careless mistake.
D. There is no mistake about the news.

76. A. She does not want to part in her house.
B. She parted her hair in the middle.
C. He will take part in the singing contest.
D. On my part, I am for the proposal.

77. A. He was writing all the while.
B. She likes to while away afternoons.
C. He visits his grandparents once a while.
D. Some students like math, while others like music.

78. A. We should not start a war at all costs.
B. The cost of living is going up.
C. The hotel room costs $300 per night.
D. She traveled around the world in a cost of her parents.

79. A. Luckily his house escaped the fire.
B. I always check for an escape route at a hotel.
C. The prisoner made his escape.
D. She had narrow escape from the flood.

80. A. Would you do the honors at the wedding party?
B. He had the honor of being selected for the best writer's award.
C. She graduated from the university with honor.
D. He honors his teachers who supported him.

IX. 次の英文を読み、設問の答として最も適切なものをA、B、C、Dの中から1つ選びなさい。

South Korea launched a rocket carrying a moon *orbit satellite on Thursday, August 5, 2022. Originally known as the Korea *Pathfinder *Lunar Orbiter, the mission was given the name “Danuri” after it became the winning entry in a naming contest. It joins the Korean words for “moon” and “enjoy.”

“We are also considering using the moon as an *outpost for space exploration,” said Kwon Hyun-joon, director general of space and nuclear energy at South Korea’s Ministry of Science, adding: “Although we hope to explore the moon itself, we also recognize its potential to act as a base for further deep space exploration such as Mars and beyond.”

Danuri was launched from Florida, setting out on a *roundabout but fuel-efficient path to the moon. It will enter the moon’s orbit in December 2022 at an altitude of about 100 kilometers above the surface. The main mission is scheduled to last for one year.

Danuri will join spacecraft from the U.S. and India already operating around the moon, and a China *rover exploring the moon’s far side. Danuri’s mission includes searching for a future landing site and testing space Internet technology, South Korea’s science ministry said.

The spacecraft’s scientific *payload will aid scientists in South Korea and around the world in studying the moon’s magnetic field, measuring its quantities of elements and molecules like uranium, water and helium-3 and photographing craters at the lunar poles, where the sun never shines.

One of Danuri’s most important scientific instruments is a *magnetometer. The moon’s interior no longer generates a magnetic field, but it once did, and that ancient field is preserved in *lava flows that hardened during that time. The moon’s early magnetic field appears to have been surprisingly strong, possibly as much as double the strength of Earth’s current magnetic field.

注）*orbit 軌道　*pathfinder 探査衛星　*lunar orbiter 月周回衛星
*outpost 前哨基地　*roundabout 回り道の、遠回りの　*rover 探査車
*payload 観測機器　*magnetometer 磁力計　*lava 溶岩

81.　What does the name “Danuri” mean?

A.　Enjoy the moon.　　B.　Let’s go to the moon together.
C.　The moon will enjoy Danuri.　　D.　Roundabout fuel efficiency.

82. Who is Kwon Hyun-joon?

A. The President of Korea.
B. A journalist.
C. An astronaut.
D. A director general.

83. What is the South Korean Ministry's immediate objective regarding the moon?

A. Start a space colony on the moon.
B. Make the satellite last for two years.
C. Making a roundabout but fuel-efficient path to the moon.
D. Having Danuri return to Earth after its mission is done.

84. What is one of Danuri's main jobs?

A. Danuri will help people already on the moon.
B. Danuri will join a spacecraft from Japan.
C. Danuri will land on the moon.
D. Danuri will test space Internet technology.

85. What other countries are exploring the moon according to the text?

A. France and Germany.
B. Japan and Taiwan.
C. India and Russia.
D. China and India.

86. Name one thing that Danuri will help scientists to understand the moon.

A. Looking for past life on the moon.
B. Finding oceans on the moon.
C. Photographing craters at the moon's poles.
D. Learning to live on the moon.

87. What is one important thing mentioned about the moon's poles?

A. The poles are the warmest parts of the moon.
B. The sun never shines on the lunar poles.
C. Magnetism on the moon is weakest at the poles.
D. People lived on the poles.

88. What do we know about the history of the moon's magnetic field?

A. The magnetic field is strong now but it was weak in the past.
B. The magnetic field was strong in the past, but it is gone now.
C. The magnetic field is different on different parts of the moon.
D. Scientists know very little about the moon's magnetic field.

89. What do we know about the moon's magnetic field in the past?

A. The moon's magnetic field was twice as strong as Earth's current one.

B. There are no hardened lava flows on the moon.

C. Once Earth went around the moon.

D. Ancient people saw volcanos on the moon.

90. What is the best title for this story?

A. Danuri Will Land on the Moon!

B. Danuri Will Return from the Moon!

C. Danuri Will Orbit the Moon!

D. Danuri Will Crash into the Moon!

X. 次の会話を読み、設問の答として最も適切なものをA、B、C、Dの中から1つ選びなさい。

Taro : It's extremely hot this summer in Japan. Is this the result of climate change?

Yoko : I prefer "global warming." It's more *straightforward than "climate change," which might make people feel that rising temperatures aren't so dangerous, or even their problem.

Taro : Well sure, some problems are not our problems. We're not having huge forest fires here in Japan like in France or California.

Yoko : That's what's wrong with people when they don't see that their problems are connected to ours. We are having terrible floods and that is caused by climate change, that is global warming.

Taro : You mean floods and forest fires are caused by climate change? I can't imagine it!

Yoko : That's what makes global warming so dangerous. People do not see connections.

Taro : Do you know outdated women's fashion clothes are thrown on huge heaps that rot and increase the Earth's temperature?

Yoko : **(95)** I knew that was coming! For your information, many women are fighting against male-run clothing companies that are careless with the Earth's ecology. Women are redesigning old clothes or giving them to poor people. But what you just brought up is not among the worst climate problems. The major problems are connected to overproduction and waste. Because of that, the Earth is getting increasingly hotter and *ecological systems are suffering.

Taro : What's the future going to be like? I'm scared our ecological systems will collapse.

Yoko : You are not alone. The late Stephan Hawking was worried that the Earth would become so hot that people would need to search for other *habitable planets.

Taro : There is no other habitable planet that we know!

Yoko : That's why our most important job is to save the Earth's ecology.

注）*straightforward 単刀直入な 率直な *ecological system 生態系
*habitable 居住可能な、住める

91. Why does Yoko prefer to use "global warming" to "climate change"?

A. She doesn't like the changes of seasons.

B. She likes warm climates better than cold ones.

C. It's more precise in defining our ecological crisis.

D. It sounds cute.

92. What does Taro think about forest fires in France?

A. They are dangerous.

B. They are Yoko's problem.

C. They are not caused by global warming.

D. They are not his problem.

93. What else does Yoko say is a problem caused by global warming, besides huge forest fires?

A. Terrible floods.

B. People who are not indifferent to global problems.

C. A sudden drop of the Earth's temperature.

D. There is not enough clothes.

94. What does Taro think about terrible floods?

A. He thinks they are only Japan's problem.

B. He cannot imagine that they are caused by global warming.

C. He does not care about them.

D. He thinks they are connected to global warming.

95. What does Yoko mean by (95) "I knew that was coming!"?

A. She expected Taro would blame women's clothes.

B. She knew Taro was to blame for thrown away clothes.

C. She anticipated Taro would come to see her.

D. She knew the old clothes would be delivered to her soon.

96. What does Yoko say about women regarding male-run clothing companies?

A. Women are supporting companies to make more profits.

B. Women are fighting against careless clothing companies that hurt the Earth's ecology.

C. Women are happy with companies because they get promotions.

D. Women are not interested in companies' policies because they have nothing to do with them.

97. What are women doing about outdated women's clothes?

A. They are selling them to make profits.

B. They are burning them to get rid of them.

C. They are redesigning them or giving them to people in need.

D. They are piling them up and letting them rot.

98. What does Yoko say about major problems connected to climate change?

A. Too many people care about climate change.

B. Not enough things to sell and buy.

C. Connecting climate change to people's under consumption.

D. Overproduction and waste.

99. What does Yoko say about the influences of global warming?

A. More women are getting rid of their outdated clothes.

B. People are afraid of living without money.

C. There are less people who think global warming affects ecological systems.

D. The Earth is getting hotter and ecological systems are suffering.

100. What was the late Stephan Hawking's concern?

A. The Earth would become so hot that people would need to find other livable planets.

B. The Earth would be occupied by people from other planets.

C. People would worry about the Earth's ecological systems too much.

D. People would lose interest in making money when the Earth became too hot.

マークシート記入例

東京の本会場でC級を受験する、国連 太郎さん、受験番号が「東京01-40001」、生年月日が「1980年10月24日」の場合の記入例です。

【受験番号/氏名】
それぞれ受験票の記載通りに記入してください。

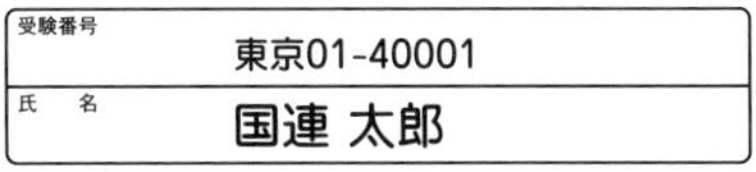

【受験地区】
下段の都道府県部分を塗りつぶしてください。

【会場番号】
都道府県部分に続く２桁の数字を塗りつぶしてください。

【受験番号】
ハイフン（－）以降の５桁の数字を塗りつぶしてください。

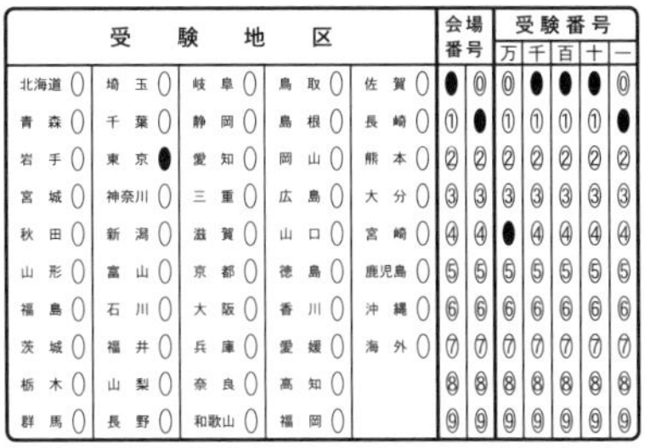

【受験級】
「C」と記入し、下段のC級部分を塗りつぶしてください。

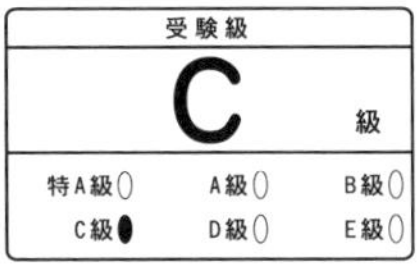

【生年月日】
４桁の西暦・月・日を塗りつぶしてください。
10未満の月・日の十の位は、「０」を塗りつぶしてください。

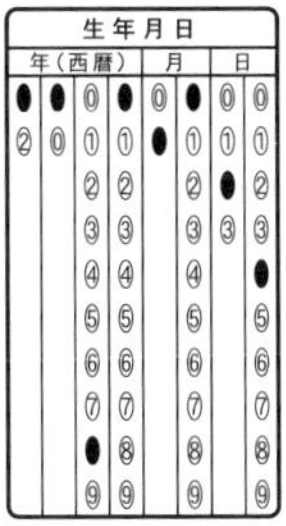

※HB以上の鉛筆を用いてマークをしてください。

※他の地区から会場を変更して受験する場合でも、受験票に記載されている受験地区・会場番号をマークしてください。

2022年

第2回試験

解答・解説

2022年　国連英検C級第2回試験
解答・解説

I　短い英文を2度聴いたあと，
その英文に対して適切な応答を選ぶリスニングテスト。10問出題。

1.　解答：C

解説　話者は相手に明日までに手紙を郵送してほしいと依頼しているので，選択肢の中で最もふさわしい応答は，Cが正解。

ナレーション　Could you mail this letter by tomorrow?
「この手紙を明日までに郵送してもらえますか」

A. 私は明日，彼に会います。　B. 彼はよくわからないようです。
C. 私はきょうそれを郵送します。　D. 私は昨日郵便局へ行きました。

2.　解答：A

解説　話者は相手に会議の準備をしなければならないと伝えているので，選択肢の中で最もふさわしい応答は，Aが正解。

ナレーション　I must prepare for the meeting.
「私は会議の準備をしなければなりません」

A. 参加人数は何人ですか。　B. 私は会議に遅刻しそうです。
C. 部屋には誰もいません。　D. 彼女は会議に出席しませんでした。

3.　解答：D

解説　話者は，相手の好きなことは読書なのかと確認しているので，選択肢の中で最もふさわしい応答は，Dが正解。

ナレーション　You like to read, don't you?
「読書が好きなんですね」

A. 私は幸せな気分です。　B. あなたは歌いたいとは思いませんか。
C. あなたは趣味がありますか。　D. 私は読書が大好きです。

4. 解答：B

解説 話者は相手に運動する頻度を尋ねているので，選択肢の中で最もふさわしい応答は，B が正解。

ナレーション How often do you exercise?

「あなたはどのくらいの頻度で運動しますか」

A. あなたは走ることが好きですか。

B. 私に時間があるときならいつでも。

C. 私は変化が欲しいです。

D. 私は先週ジョギングをしました。

5. 解答：A

解説 話者は相手にバスが遅れた理由を知りたいと伝えているので，選択肢の中で最もふさわしい応答は，A が正解。

ナレーション Please tell me why the bus was delayed.

「バスが遅れた理由を教えてください」

A. 道路が混んでいました。　B. 私はタクシーに乗りました。

C. 誰もバスに乗りませんでした。　D. 運転手は近道をしました。

6. 解答：C

解説 話者は相手にコンサートの開始時刻を尋ねているので，選択肢の中で最もふさわしい応答は，C が正解。

ナレーション When will the concert begin?

「コンサートはいつ始まるのですか」

A. 私はあなたにロビーでお会いしましょう。

B. 私は友達をたくさん連れてきます。

C. 今夜，8 時に。

D. 昨夜，7 時に。

7. 解答：B

解説 話者は相手に言葉の意味を知りたいときの手段について尋ねているので，選択肢の中で最もふさわしい応答は，B が正解。

ナレーション What do you do to learn the meaning of a word?

「言葉の意味を知るために，どんなことをしますか」

A. 私は音楽を聴きます。　B. 私は辞書を調べます。
C. 私は友人と外出します。　D. 私は家族と料理をします。

8. 解答：C

解説　話者は相手に明日のテストのため頑張っていると伝えているので，選択肢の中で最もふさわしい応答は，C が正解。

ナレーション　I'm working hard for the test tomorrow.
「明日のテストに向けて頑張っています」

A. 私は疲れました。
B. 私はお腹が空いています。
C. テストは何についてですか。
D. あなたはなぜ頑張っているのですか。

9. 解答：D

解説　話者は相手に有名な画家の無料展覧会に行ったと伝えているので，選択肢の中で最もふさわしい応答は，D が正解。

ナレーション　I went to the famous painter's free exhibition yesterday.
「昨日，有名な画家の無料展覧会に行きました」

A. ずっと風が強いです。
B. 私は道に迷いました。
C. 美術館の入場料は高かったです。
D. 私は彼の評判を聞いたことがあります。

10. 解答：A

解説　話者は相手に黒インクカートリッジが必要だと伝えているので，選択肢の中で最もふさわしい応答は，A が正解。

ナレーション　I desperately need to buy a black ink cartridge for my printer, but the store is closed now.
「プリンターの黒インクカートリッジをどうしても買いたいのですが，お店はもう閉まっています」

A. あなたのために予備があります。　B. よかったね。
C. じゃあ，食事に行きましょう。　D. お店は遠いです。

II 短い会話を２度聴いたあと，その内容に関する質問を聴いて答えるリスニングテスト。10問出題。

11. 解答：B

解説 男性は万年筆の修理屋さんを知っていると言っている。Bが正解。

A. 男性は万年筆の修理の仕方を知っています。

B. 男性は万年筆を修理できる人を知っています。

C. そのペンは優れているので，いますぐ使えるはずです。

D. そのペンは壊れているので，もう二度と使えないでしょう。

ナレーション

Woman: My fountain pen doesn't work anymore.

Man: I know an excellent fountain pen repair person.

Question　What does the man mean?

(女)：私の万年筆が使えなくなったわ。

(男)：腕がいい万年筆の修理屋さんを知っていますよ。

質問　男性は何と言っていますか。

12. 解答：D

解説 女性は男性に日本での仕事が決まったことがうれしいと言っている。Dが正解。

A. 彼女は興奮していません。

B. 彼女は何をしたらいいかわかりません。

C. 彼女はすでに日本で仕事をしています。

D. 彼女は日本で働くのが待ちきれない。

ナレーション

Man: Congratulations! You got that job in Japan.

Woman: I'm simply overwhelmed!

Question　What does the woman mean?

(男)：おめでとう。日本での仕事が決まったんだね。

(女)：とてもワクワクしているわ。

質問　女性は何と言っていますか。

13. 解答：A

解説 男性は女性の車の修理が終わっていないと言っている。Aが正解。

A. 彼女の車はまだ修理が必要です。

B. 彼女はすぐに車を引き取りに行きます。

C. 彼女は車を売るでしょう。

D. 彼女の車は高価です。

ナレーション

Woman: I'll pick up my car before going on vacation.

Man: But the car still needs more work.

Question What does the man mean?

(女)：休暇に入る前に車を引き取りに行きます。

(男)：でも車はまだ修理が必要なんだ。

質問 男性は何と言っていますか。

14. 解答：C

解説 女性は男性に仕事の選択は個人の自由だと言っている。C が正解。

A. 彼らは間違った仕事に就いています。

B. 男性と女性の仕事は違うはずです。

C. どんな仕事に就いてもいいのです。

D. その女性は服飾デザイナーになりたいと思っています。

ナレーション

Man: When I said I'm a dress designer, my friends laughed.

Woman: I understand your feelings. I drive a truck.

Question What does the woman mean?

(男)：僕が服飾デザイナーだと言ったら，友達に笑われたよ。

(女)：あなたの気持ちはよくわかるわ。私はトラックの運転手なの。

質問 女性は何と言っていますか。

15. 解答：A

解説 男性は女性に申し立てをするように言っている。file a complaint は「告訴する」の意味。A が正解。

A. 女性は法的措置を求めるべきです。

B. その女性はマネージャーに昼食をおごるべきです。

C. その女性は個人的に問題を解決する必要があります。

D. 女性はマネージャーに謝るべきです。

ナレーション

Woman: My manager harassed me. What should I do?

Man: File a complaint!

Question What does the man mean?

(女)：マネージャーから嫌がらせを受けたの。どうしたらいいかしら。

(男)：苦情申し立てをしたらいいのに。

質問 男性は何と言っていますか。

16. 解答：B

解説 女性は男性に好き嫌いに関係なく追加接種は必要だと言っている。B が正解。

A. 追加接種を受けるかどうかは彼の自由です。

B. 彼女は追加接種を必要不可欠だと考えています。

C. 彼女は追加接種は危険だと考えています。

D. 彼らは追加接種を受けるのを延期することに賛成です。

ナレーション

Man: I am tired of having booster shots for COVID. What's the use?

Woman: You need those boosters, like it or not.

Question What does the woman mean?

(男)：新型コロナウイルス感染症の追加接種はもう飽きたよ。何になるんだろう。

(女)：好き嫌いに関係なく，追加接種は必要よ。

質問 女性は何と言っていますか。

17. 解答：C

解説 男性は，わざわざ熱波の予想される国々に行くことについて女性からの批判を，アイスランドで涼むとユーモアで返している。C が正解。

A. 彼は夏場に暑いヨーロッパ諸国を避けるでしょう。

B. 彼は夏が涼しいアイスランドにしか行かないでしょう。

C. 彼は暑いヨーロッパの国々を訪問し，その後アイスランドを訪問するでしょう。

D. どちらとも言えません。

ナレーション

Woman: You're crazy to fly to Europe in summer with the expected heat waves.

Man: I'll cool off in Iceland later.

Question　What does the man mean?

(女)：熱波が予想される夏のヨーロッパに飛ぶなんて，どうかしているわ。

(男)：あとで，アイスランドで涼むよ。

質問　男性は何と言っていますか。

18.　解答：A

解説　女性は画家からその絵をもらったと言っている。A が正解。

A. 彼女は画家から絵をもらいました。

B. 彼女はその絵を買いました。

C. 彼女はその絵を自宅のガレージで見つけました。

D. 彼女はその絵を盗みました。

ナレーション

Man: How could you have gotten this famous painting?

Woman: The painter gave it to me.

Question　What does the woman mean?

(男)：どうしてこんな有名な絵が手に入ったの？

(女)：画家がくれたのよ。

質問　女性は何と言っていますか。

19.　解答：D

解説　男性はテーブルを動かして欲しいという依頼に対してもちろんいいですよと言っている。by all means は「もちろん，よろしいですとも」の意味。D が正解。

A. 彼はやりたくありません。　B. 彼は病気です。

C. 彼はいま忙しいです。　D. 彼は喜んで彼女を助けるでしょう。

ナレーション

Woman: Could you help me move this table?

Man: By all means.

Question　What does the man mean?
(女)：このテーブルを動かすのを手伝ってもらえますか。
(男)：もちろんだよ。
質問　男性は何と言っていますか。

20.　解答：C

解説　女性は男性に好きなだけコーヒーを飲めると言っている。C が正解。
A. 彼女はコーヒーを切らしています。
B. 彼女はコーヒーが少ししか残っていません。
C. 彼は好きなだけコーヒーを飲むことができます。
D. 彼はコーヒーの代金を支払わなければなりません。

ナレーション

Man:　　May I have another cup of coffee?
Woman: You can have all the coffee you want.
Question　What does the woman mean?
(男)：コーヒーをもう 1 杯いただけますか。
(女)：好きなだけ飲んでください。
質問　女性は何と言っていますか。

III

まとまりのある内容の英文（300 語前後）を 2 度聴いたあと，
その内容に関する英語の質問を聴いて答えるリスニングテスト。10 問出題。

21.　解答：B

解説　“Jean was worried as darkness in their small village increased.” から，正解は B。
A. 街に　　B. 小さな村に　　C. トレーラーパークに　　D. 集合住宅に

22.　解答：C

解説　“She had called his cellphone. When he didn’t answer, she contacted the Highway Patrol.” から，正解は C。
A. 彼女は道に迷った。
B. 彼女は飼っている動物を見つけることができなかった。
C. 彼女は携帯電話で夫と連絡を取ることができなかった。
D. 彼女の夫が彼女に怒っていた。

23. 解答：B

解説 "An hour later they called to say they had not found her husband." から，正解は B。

A. 彼らは夫を見つけた。

B. 彼らは彼女の夫を見つけられなかった。

C. 彼女の夫のジャックはハイウェーパトロールに電話した。

D. ハイウェーパトロールが犬と猫を連れて行った。

24. 解答：B

解説 "'I'm going to find Jack myself,' Jean said." から，正解は B。

A. 犬や猫と一緒にジャックを捜す。

B. 1 人でジャックを探す。

C. 犬と猫を家から追い出す。

D. 犬と猫をハイウェーパトロールに渡す。

25. 解答：D

解説 "The dog and cat barked and meowed. Finally, she let them into the car." から，正解は D。

A. 2 匹は家に残った。

B. ジーンは 2 匹を外に残して車を走らせた。

C. 彼らは車を避けた。

D. 彼らは車の中でジーンと一緒にいたいという気持ちを表した。

26. 解答：C

解説 "Sit in the back seat, creatures, and don't bother me," she said. から，正解は C。

A.「喧嘩しないでね」と彼女は叫んだ。

B.「私のことは心配しないでね」と彼女は言った。

C. 彼女は彼らに後部座席で静かにするように言った。

D. 彼女は彼らに前の座席に座るように言った。

27. 解答：C

解説 "Jean's first thought was to drive to the hardware store." から，正解

は C。

A. 彼女は自分が何をしているのかわからなかった。

B. 彼女は家にいたかった。

C. 彼女は金物屋に行こうと考えた。

D. 彼女はハイウェーパトロールに車を走らせようと思った。

28. 解答：A

解説 “The animals grew louder and put their paws on her shoulders.” から，正解は A。

A. 彼らはジーンが止めるように言ったのに，吠《ほ》えたり，叫んだりした。

B. 彼らはハイウェーパトロールのことをジーンに警告した。

C. 彼らはけんかを始めた。

D. ジーンがドアを開けると，彼らはジーンから逃げ出した。

29. 解答：D

解説 “She nearly scolded the dog and cat when she heard a familiar voice. Her husband was calling from behind some trees on an almost hidden narrow road. She remembered him telling her there was a narrow shortcut to the city.” から，正解は D。

A. ハイウェーパトロールがジャックを救った。

B. 犬と猫が金物屋への近道を思い出させた。

C. 聞き覚えのある声がジーンを呼んだ。

D. B と C の両方が正しい。

30. 解答：B

解説 “His car had run off the road and the engine had stopped.” から，正解は B。

A. ジャックはガス欠になった。

B. 車は道路から外れて壊れた。

C. ジャックは道に迷った。

D. ハイウェーパトロールがジャックを逮捕した。

ナレーション

Jean was worried as darkness in their small village increased. Her husband, Jack, who had gone shopping to the city hardware store, should have been home hours ago. She had called his cellphone. When he didn't answer, she contacted the Highway Patrol. An hour later they called to say they had not found her husband.

Their dog and cat — Spotty and Tiger — were as worried as Jean.

"I'm going to find Jack myself," Jean said. Spotty and Tiger were at her heels.

"You two stay home!" Jean declared.

The dog and cat barked and meowed. Finally, she let them into the car. "Sit in the back seat, creatures, and don't bother me," she said. Actually, she was happy to have them as she was nervous about deciding what to do.

Jean's first thought was to drive to the hardware store. As she was driving, the dog and cat started to bark and yowl.

"Quiet!" she said.

The animals grew louder and put their paws on her shoulders. She braked and stopped. She nearly scolded the dog and cat when she heard a familiar voice. Her husband was calling from behind some trees on an almost hidden narrow road. She remembered him telling her there was a narrow shortcut to the city.

Jean blew the horn. Immediately Jack appeared and called her name.

On the way home, as the cat and dog slept, he told Jean what had happened. His car had run off the road and the engine had stopped. Somehow his cellphone broke. He thought he might get lost in the dark and decided to stay in the car until morning.

"I'm so glad you figured out where to find me," he said.

"Thank our dog and cat," she said.

Questions 21. Where did Jean and her husband, Jack, live?

22. Why was Jean worried?

23. What happened after Jean called the Highway Patrol?

24. What did Jean decide to do first?
25. What did the dog and cat finally do?
26. What did Jean do or say in the car?
27. What was Jean’s plan to find Jack?
28. What did the dog and cat do while she was driving?
29. How did Jean and Jack find each other?
30. What had happened to Jack’s car on the narrow shortcut?

訳例　ジーンは，小さな村の暗闇が広がる中で心配していた。街の金物屋に買い物に行った夫のジャックは，何時間も前に帰宅しているはずだった。彼女は夫の携帯電話に電話をかけた。夫が電話に出なかったので彼女はハイウェーパトロールに連絡した。1時間後，パトカーから電話があり，夫は見つかっていないとのことだった。

犬のスポッティと猫のタイガーも，ジーンと同じように心配していた。

「自分でジャックを見つけるわ」とジーンは言った。スポッティとタイガーは，彼女の後を追いかけた。

「あなたたち２匹とも家にいるのよ」とジーンがきっぱりと言った。

犬は吠え，猫はニャーと鳴いた。結局，彼女は彼らを車の中に入れた。「あなたたちは後部座席に座って，私を困らせないでね」と彼女は言った。実は，どうしたらいいのか決めるのが不安だったので，この２匹を車に乗せて彼女はよかったと思った。

ジーンはまず，金物屋に行こうと考えた。彼女が運転をしていたら，犬と猫が鳴き始めた。

「静かにして！」と彼女は言った。

動物たちはもっと大声で鳴き出し，彼女の肩に前足を乗せた。彼女はブレーキをかけ止まった。彼女が犬や猫を叱りそうになったとき，聞き覚えのある声を耳にした。夫が木の陰から，ほとんど人目につかない細い道で呼んでいた。彼女は夫が街へ行くのに近道があると言っていたのを思い出した。

ジーンがクラクションを鳴らした。すぐにジャックが現れ，彼女の名前を呼んだ。

帰り道，猫と犬が寝ている間に，彼は起こったことをジーンに話した。彼の車は道路から外れてエンジンが止まってしまった。なぜか彼の携帯電話も壊れた。彼は暗闇で道に迷うかもしれないと思い，朝まで車の中にいることにした。

「僕を見つけてくれて本当にうれしいよ」と彼は言った。

「うちの犬と猫に感謝してね」と彼女が言った。

質問　21. ジーンと夫のジャックはどこに住んでいましたか。

22. ジーンはなぜ心配したのですか。

23. ジーンがハイウェーパトロールに電話した後，何が起こりましたか。

24. ジーンはまず何をしようと思いましたか。

25. 犬と猫は結局どうしましたか。

26. 車の中でジーンは何をし，または何を言いましたか。

27. ジャックを見つけるために，ジーンはどんな計画を立てましたか。

28. 彼女が運転している間，犬と猫は何をしましたか。

29. ジーンとジャックはどうやってお互いを見つけましたか。

30. ジャックの車は狭い近道でどうなったのですか。

IV 会話を２度聴いたあと，
その内容に関する英語の質問を聴いて答えるリスニングテスト。10 問出題。

31.　解答：A

解説 マリアンヌが“I'm sad, George. My favorite local bookstore closed.”と言っていることから，正解は A。

A. 彼女の好きな本屋が閉店した。

B. 彼女は本を全部なくしてしまった。

C. 彼女は孤独だ。

D. 彼女はお腹が空いている。

32.　解答：B

解説 マリアンヌが“It not only had great new and used books, but also a coffeeshop where we had poetry readings.”と言っていることから，正解は B。

A. 食料品　　B. コーヒーショップと詩の朗読

C. 電化製品　　D. コンピューター

33.　解答：D

解説 ジョージが“Now we can get books quickly through the Internet. Look at the time we save in searching for books!”と言っていることから，正解は D。

A. コーヒーとケーキ　B. ライブの詩の朗読
C. 有名な詩人との握手　D. 本を探す時間の短縮

34. 解答：A

解説 マリアンヌが “I came up with some unexpectedly great books.” と言っていることから，正解は A。
A. 素晴らしい本　B. 鉛筆と消しゴム　C. 電子書籍　D. 花

35. 解答：B

解説 ジョージが “And no more old books taking up space in my house.” と言っていることから，正解は B。
A. それらはあなたの家では素敵に見えます。
B. それらは場所を取らない。
C. それらは目に優しい。
D. それらは高価に見える。

36. 解答：A

解説 ジョージが “You can publish your own book electronically.” と言っていることから，正解は A。
A. 自分の本を電子出版することが可能である。
B. 作家は多くの紙を使わなければならない。
C. インターネット作家は必ず金持ちになる。
D. 電子出版はほとんど不可能だ。

37. 解答：B

解説 ジョージが “Not only would books disappear but artwork as well.” と言っていることから，正解は B。
A. 何も起こらないだろう。
B. 私たちの電子情報はすべて破壊される可能性がある。
C. 電子書籍だけが消滅する可能性がある。
D. ハードコピーの本が消えるだろう。

38. 解答：C

解説 ジョージが“All the photographs I've uploaded on my website would be no more!” と言っていることから，正解は C。

A. 散歩　B. お菓子作り　C. 写真撮影　D. 音楽

39. 解答：A

解説 マリアンヌが“The loss I feel the most now is the end of our local used bookstore.” と言っていることから，正解は A。

A. 近所の古本屋さん　B. インターネットの本屋さん

C. 彼女の好きなレストラン　D. ロックミュージック

40. 解答：B

解説 マリアンヌとジョージの会話全体を通して，伝統的な書店とインターネット書店について話をしていることから，正解は B。

A. インターネットを通じて金持ちになる

B. 伝統的な書店 対 インターネットの書店

C. 書店で喫茶店を経営する方法

D. ホームメイドクッキーの作り方

ナレーション

Marianne: I'm sad, George. My favorite local bookstore closed. It not only had great new and used books, but also a coffeeshop where we had poetry readings.

George: I miss that old bookstore too, Marianne. But there are lots of great new alternatives to traditional bookstores. Now we can get books quickly through the Internet. Look at the time we save in searching for books!

Marianne: I remember the pleasure of taking hours to look through old books. I came up with some unexpectedly great books.

George: Well, I do miss the coffeeshop and the famous and local poets who read to us. That's something the Internet cannot replace. On the other hand, I have electronic books that I got for a fraction of the cost of paper books. And no more old books taking up space in my house.

Marianne: I somehow like a lot of books around me.

George: There is another thing. You can publish your own book electronically.

Marianne: But what happens if there is a disaster in the future when all our electronic information is wiped out and there are no hard copies anymore?

George: That is truly a terrible thought. Not only would books disappear but artwork as well. All the photographs I've uploaded on my website would be no more!

Marianne: The loss I feel the most now is the end of our local used bookstore. I miss the friendly atmosphere and the classical music. And I miss the homemade cookies and cakes too!

George: Yes, I miss all of that! Can we not start our own coffeeshop and bookstore?

Marianne: Only in our dreams. But maybe someone will establish a new bookstore like the one we lost.

Questions 31. Why is Marianne sad?

32. What else did the bookstore have besides books?

33. What does George like about the Internet bookstores?

34. What did Marianne find in traditional bookstores?

35. What is good about electronic books?

36. What is one new advantage for writers regarding the Internet?

37. What could happen if there was a world-wide electronic disaster?

38. What is George's hobby?

39. What does Marianne miss most?

40. What is the best title for this conversation?

訳例　マリアンヌ：悲しいわ，ジョージ。私のお気に入りの地元の書店が閉店してしまったの。新刊や古本が充実していただけでなく，コーヒーショップもあって，詩の朗読会もやっていたのよ。

ジョージ：　僕もその古い書店が恋しいよ，マリアンヌ。でも，伝統的な書店に代わる新しくて素晴らしい書店がたくさんあるんだ。いまはインターネットですぐに本を手に入れることができる。本を探す時間が短縮されたことを考えてみて。

マリアンヌ：何時間もかけて古い本に目を通すのが楽しみだったのを思い出すわ。思いがけず，いい本と出会えたわ。

ジョージ：　コーヒーショップで，有名な詩人や地元の詩人が朗読してくれたことは，とても懐かしいなぁ。あれはインターネットでは代替できないからね。一方，電子書籍は紙の書籍の何分の1かのコストで手に入れることができるんだ。それに家の中で場所をとる古い本もなくなったしね。

マリアンヌ：私はなんとなく，自分の周りに本がたくさんあるのが好きだわ。

ジョージ：　もう1つあるんだよ。自分の本を電子出版することができるんだ。

マリアンヌ：でも，もし将来，大災害が起きて，私たちの電子情報がすべて消去され，ハードコピーがなくなったらどうなるのかしら。

ジョージ：　それは本当に恐ろしいことだな。本だけでなく，芸術作品も消えてしまう。僕がウェブサイトにアップロードした写真もすべてなくなってしまうってことだね。

マリアンヌ：私のいま一番の喪失感は，地元の古本屋がなくなってしまったことなの。親しみやすい雰囲気とクラシック音楽が懐かしいわ。それに，手作りのクッキーやケーキもね。

ジョージ：　そうだね，すべてが懐かしいよ。自分たちでコーヒーショップと本屋を始められないかな。

マリアンヌ：夢の中だけね。でも，私たちが失った書店のような新しい書店を誰かが作ってくれるかもしれないわね。

質問　31. なぜマリアンヌは悲しんでいるのですか。

32. 本屋には，本以外に何がありましたか。

33. ジョージはインターネットの本屋のどこが好きですか。

34. マリアンヌは従来の書店で何を見つけましたか。

35. 電子書籍のいいところは何ですか。

36. 作家にとって，インターネットに関する新しい利点は何ですか。

37. 世界的な電子災害が起きたらどうなりますか。

38. ジョージの趣味は何ですか。

39. マリアンヌがいちばん恋しいものは何ですか。

40. この会話に最も適切なタイトルは何ですか。

V 英文の下線部の意味を最もよく表す語または語句を4つの選択肢中から1つ選ぶ問題。10問出題。

41. 解答：C

解説 lose one's shirt in (on) は「(ギャンブルなどで) 無一文になる」の意味なので，C が正解。

訳例 彼は株を買って無一文になった。

A. 驚くほどの金持ちになった　B. 服をなくしてしまった
C. とても貧乏になった　D. クリーニング屋をやめた

42. 解答：A

解説 You are more than welcome. は歓迎を表す「あなたは非常に歓迎されている」，お礼の言葉に対して，より丁寧に答える「どういたしまして」の意味なので，A が正解。

訳例 あなたはとても歓迎されています。

A. 非常に歓迎される　B. 歓迎されない
C. 信じられないほど疲れた　D. 無事に到着した

43. 解答：D

解説 role model は「模範，お手本」の意味なので，D が正解。

訳例 彼女はクラスのお手本です。

A. ファッションデザイナー　B. 教師
C. 芸術家　D. 優等生

44. 解答：B

解説 be embarrassed to death は「死ぬほど恥ずかしい，とても恥ずかしい」の意味なので，B が正解。

訳例 私は死ぬほど恥ずかしかった。

A. ショックで入院した　B. ひどく恥ずかしかった
C. 殺されそうになった　D. あなたを笑ってばかりいた

45. 解答：B

解説 beside oneself は「我を忘れて」の意味なので，B が正解。

訳例 ダブリンに戻れたことをとてもうれしく思っています。

A. ゾッとした　B. とてもうれしい　C. 困惑している　D. 無関心な

46. 解答：B

解説 as smooth as glass は「ガラスのように滑らかな，とても穏やかな」の意味なので，B が正解。

訳例 今日の海はガラスのように滑らかだ。

A. 荒い　B. とても穏やかな　C. とてもきれい　D. 危険な

47. 解答：C

解説 writer's block は「(作家などの) 創作の行き詰まり (書けなくなるスランプ状態)」の意味なので，C が正解。

訳例 彼女は最近，執筆の行き詰まりを抱えている。

A. 幸運　B. 多くの注目　C. 執筆の問題　D. 書くことを楽しんでいる

48. 解答：A

解説 in an instant は「たちまち，すぐに」の意味なので，A が正解。

訳例 彼らは一瞬にして友情を深めた。

A. すぐに　B. 徐々に　C. 距離をおいて　D. まもなく

49. 解答：D

解説 old-fashioned は「時代遅れの，古風な」の意味なので，D が正解。

訳例 その歌はとても時代遅れだ。

A. 愚かな　B. 知的な　C. 有名な　D. 時代遅れの

50. 解答：D

解説 in those days は「その当時は」の意味なので，D が正解。

訳例 彼は当時，強かった。

A. 近頃　B. このごろ　C. 昨日　D. 昔は

VI

300～400 語程度のまとまりのある文を国連英検指定テキスト『新 わかりやすい国連の活動と世界』から抜粋し，その内容を把握しているかどうかを問う問題。10 題出題。

51. 解答：D

解説 "The Economic and Social Council (ECOSOC), which operates under the authority of the General Assembly," から，D が正解。

訳例 経済社会理事会はどのような権限で運営されているのですか。

A. 専門機関　B. 加盟国　C. 非政府組織　D. 総会

52. 解答：C

解説 “The Economic and Social Council makes recommendations and initiates activities relating to international cooperation for development,” から，C が正解。

訳例 経済社会理事会は，開発のための国際協力に関連して，どのようなことを行っていますか。

A. 会議を開催する。　B. 報告書を作成する。

C. 勧告し，活動を発議する。　D. 委員会を組織する。

53. 解答：B

解説 “The Economic and Social Council has 54 members who serve for three years,” から，B が正解。

訳例 経済社会理事会の委員の任期は何年ですか。

A. 2 年間　B. 3 年間　C. 4 年間　D. 5 年間

54. 解答：A

解説 “Voting in the Economic and Social Council is by simple majority;” から，A が正解。

訳例 経済社会理事会の採決はどのように行われますか。

A. 単純多数決で　B. 抽選で　C. えこひいきで　D. 上下関係で

55. 解答：B

解説 “The Charter of the United Nations empowers the Economic and Social Council:” から，B が正解。

訳例 経済社会理事会に人権と基本的自由の尊重を促進する権限を与えているものは何ですか。

A. 科学技術省　B. 国際連合憲章　C. 総会　D. 専門機関

56. 解答：C

解説 “This annual session used to alternate between New York and Geneva,” から，C が正解。

訳例 経済社会理事会の年次総会は，かつてどこで開催されましたか。

A. 東京とロンドン　B. サンフランシスコとパリ

C. ニューヨークとジュネーブ　D. シカゴとウィーン

57. 解答：D

解説 "Specialized agencies and related organizations also report annually to the Council." から，D が正解。

訳例 経済社会理事会に関連して，専門機関や関連機関は毎年どのような活動をしているのですか。

A. 問題を解決するための提案をする。　B. 会議の場所を提案する。

C. 会議の企画書を提出する。　D. 報告書を提出する。

58. 解答：A

解説 draft は「下書き」の意味なので，A が正解。

訳例 下線部 (58) draft はどのような意味ですか。

A. 作業途中のもの　B. 完成した作品　C. 日記　D. 対話

59. 解答：C

解説 approve は「認可する」の意味だから，C が正解。

訳例 下線部 (59) approved はどのような意味ですか。

A. 賞賛される　B. 疑問に思った　C. 許可された　D. 無視された

60. 解答：D

解説 body は「団体，組織」の意味だから，D が正解。

訳例 下線部 (60) "bodies" はどのような意味ですか。

A. 脚　B. 衣服　C. 国々　D. 組織

訳例 総会の権限のもとで機能する経済社会理事会 (ECOSOC) は，国連およびその専門機関の経済社会活動を調整するための機関である。経済社会理事会は，開発，世界貿易，産業化，天然資源，人権，女性の地位，人口，社会福祉，教育，保健およびその関連分野，社会技術，犯罪の防止，麻薬取締まり，その他の経済社会問題における国際協力に関して勧告し，活動を発議する。

経済社会理事会は 3 年の任期を持つ 54 カ国で構成される。毎年，任期の切れる 3 分の 1 の 18 カ国に代わって，新たに 18 カ国が 3 年の任期で選出される。

経済社会理事会の表決は単純多数決であり，各理事国が 1 票を持つ。国連憲章は経済社会理事会に主として次のような権限を与えている。

- 経済，社会，文化，教育および保健に関連する問題に関する研究を行い，国際行動の必要性を勧告する。

- 人権および基本的自由の尊重を推進する。
- その権限に属する事項について国際会議を招集し，総会に提出する条約の草案を作成する。
- 専門機関との間で，各機関と国連との連帯関係の条件に関する取り決めを結び，各機関の活動を調整する。
- 総会の承認を得た加盟国に対して，また専門機関からの要請に対して，役務を提供する。
- その権限内にある事項に関係ある民間団体との協議にあたる。

経済社会理事会は通常毎年1回，通常会期をニューヨークとジュネーブにおいて交互に開催していたが，現在は，人道支援部門を除き，毎年ニューヨークで開催している。

経済社会理事会の年間を通じての活動は地域委員会や機能委員会などによって推進されている。専門機関・関連機関も経済社会理事会に，毎年定期報告を行う。

『新 わかりやすい国連の活動と世界』pp. 56–57

Ⅶ

2つの文章に共通して用いられる語を1つ，選択肢の中から選ぶ問題。
10問出題。

61. 解答：C

解説 smartは形容詞で「賢明な，知能の高い」と「(打撃などが) 強烈な」の意味。正解はC。

訳例 「彼女は賢い学生だ」
「その一撃は強烈だろう」
A. 明るい　B. よく　D. おいしい

62. 解答：D

解説 lateは形容詞で「今は亡き，故」，と「(時刻が) 遅い」の意味。正解はD。

訳例 「故スミス氏の栄誉が讃えられるでしょう」
「帰りが遅くなります」
A. 今　B. まもなく　C. 例年の

63. 解答：A

解説 playは他動詞で「(球技など) をする」，名詞で「劇，芝居」の意味。正解はA。

訳例　「彼女はバイオリンを弾くのが好きです」
「昨日，彼は素晴らしい芝居を見ました」
B. 命令　C. ゲーム　D. 猫

64.　解答：A

解説　spirits は名詞で「蒸留酒，火酒（ウイスキー，ブランデー，ジン，ラムなど）」と「気分」，be in good spirits で「上機嫌である」の意味。正解は A。

訳例　「彼は蒸留酒を避けなければならない」
「彼女は上機嫌です」
B. アルコール　C. 油脂　D. 笑い

65.　解答：B

解説　watch は名詞で「時計」，自動詞で「警戒する」，watch out で「用心する，警戒する」の意味。正解は B。

訳例　「彼女は腕時計を買いました」
「他の車に気をつけてください」
A. ラジオ　C. ドレス　D. ボート

66.　解答：B

解説　drive は動詞で「車を運転する」，what S is driving at で「（人）が言いたいこと」の意味。正解は B。

訳例　「あなたは何を言おうとしているのですか」
「私は車の運転が好きです」
A. 見る　C. 洗う　D. 衝突する

67.　解答：D

解説　trip は名詞で「旅」，自動詞で「つまずく」の意味。正解は D。

訳例　「あなたが今まで行った最も長い旅はどんなものですか」
「私は床に置かれたあなたのガラクタにつまずくかもしれません」
A. 晩御飯　B. 口笛　C. 犬

68.　解答：D

解説　gain は他動詞で「得る，獲得する」，gain on で「追いつく」」の意味。

正解は D。

訳例 「彼女は今年，多くのお金を稼いでいる」
「彼のレーシングカーは他のレーシングカーに追いついている」
A. 作っている　B. 負けている　C. 落ちている

69. 解答：B

解説 found は他動詞 find の過去形で「見つける」，他動詞で「を設立する」の意味。正解は B。

訳例 「彼は財布を見つけた」
「彼らは新しい政党を設立するだろう」
A. 飛ぶ　C. 運転する　D. キスする

70. 解答：C

解説 rough は形容詞で「(道などが）でこぼこの」，a rough draft で「草稿，下書き」の意味。正解は C。

訳例 「ここは道がでこぼこだ」
「本の下書きを書き上げた」
A. でこぼこの　B. 水　D. 赤ちゃん

VIII ４つの文章の中で，文法的に用法が間違っているものを見つける問題。
10 問出題。

71. 解答：A

Believe it of not → Believe it or not

「信じられないかもしれませんが，彼は大富豪なのです」

解説 believe の用法を問う問題。B の believe in は「存在を信じる」，C の make believe は「ふりをする，見せかける」，D の believe は「(人）が〜だと思う」の意味。A の下線部は「こんなことを言っても信じないだろうが」の意味なので，Believe it of not ではなく Believe it or not が正しい。A が正解。

訳例 B. あなたは神様を信じますか？
C. 私は自分が重要な人物のふりをするのは好きではありません。
D. 私は彼女が弁護士だったと思っています。

72.　解答：D

a favor to ask for → a favor to ask of

「私はあなたにお願いがあります」

解説　favor の用法を問う問題。A の in favor with は「に気に入られて」，B の come back in favor は「人気が戻る」，C の do me a favor は「私のお願いを聞く」の意味。D は「あなたにお願いがある」の意味なので，～ for (you) ではなく of (you) が正しい。D が正解。

訳例　A. 先生は生徒に気に入られています。

B. その歌手は若者の間で人気が戻ってきた。

C. 私の頼みを聞いてくれませんか。

73.　解答：B

took to his heel → took to his heels

「彼は警察官を見たとき急いで逃げた」

解説　heel の用法を問う問題。A の a heel of bread は「パンの切れ端」，C の heels は「(靴の) かかと」，D の come to heel は「服従する」の意味。B は take to one's heels で「急いで逃げる，走り去る」の意味なので，took to his heel ではなく took to his heels が正しい。B が正解。

訳例　A. テーブルの上にパンの切れ端が残っていた。

C. 彼女はヒールの高い靴を履くのが好きではない。

D. 彼の犬は彼に服従する。

74.　解答：C

in heights → in height

「彼女の身長は 5 フィートです」

解説　height の用法を問う問題。A の height は「(成功，名声，権力などの) 頂点，絶頂」in the height of one's power で「権力の絶頂期に」，B の gain height は「(飛行機) が上昇する」，D の be afraid of heights「高い所がこわい」の意味。C は「身長」の意味なので，in heights ではなく in height が正しい。C が正解。

訳例　A. 彼は権力の絶頂期にある。

B. 飛行機はゆっくりと高度を増していった。

D. 彼は高所恐怖症だ。

75.　解答：B

as mistake → by mistake

「携帯電話をうっかりして家に置いてきてしまった」

解説　mistakeの用法を問う問題。Aのmistake O forは「(人，物）を～と間違える」，Cのmake a careless mistakeは「不注意な間違いをする」，Dのno mistakeは「間違いがない」の意味。Bは「うっかりして」の意味なので，as mistakeではなくby mistakeが正しい。Bが正解。

訳例　A. 彼は私を友人と勘違いした。
C. 彼は不注意な間違いをした。
D. ニュースについて間違いはない。

76.　解答：A

part in → part with

「彼女は家を手放したくありません」

解説　partの用法を問う問題。Bのpart one's hairは「髪を真ん中で分ける」，Cのtake part inは「に参加する」，Dのon one's partは「(人）としては，(人）の側で」の意味。Aは「手放す」の意味なので，part inではなくpart withが正しい。Aが正解。

訳例　B. 彼女は髪を真ん中で分けた。
C. 彼は歌のコンテストに参加する予定です。
D. 私はこの提案に賛成です。

77.　解答：C

once a while → once in a while

「彼はときどき祖父母を訪ねる」

解説　whileの用法を問う問題。Aのall the whileは「その間中，ずっと」，Bのwhile awayは「のんびりと過ごす」，Dのwhileは「だが一方，である一方」の意味。Cはonce in a whileで「ときどき」の意味なので，once a whileではなくonce in a whileが正しい。Cが正解。

訳例　A. 彼はずっと書き続けていた。
B. 彼女は午後の時間をのんびり過ごすのが好きだ。
D. 数学が好きな生徒もいれば，音楽が好きな生徒もいる。

78. 解答：D

in a cost of → at a cost of

「彼女は両親の費用で世界中を旅行した」

解説 costの用法を問う問題。Aのat all costsは「ぜひとも，何としても」，Bのthe cost of livingは「生活費」，Cのcostは「(費用が) かかる」の意味。Dは「の費用で」の意味なので，in a cost ofではなくat a cost ofが正しい。Dが正解。

訳例 A. 何が何でも戦争を起こすべきではない。
B. 生活費が上がっている。
C. ホテルの部屋は一晩で300ドルする。

79. 解答：D

had narrow escape → had a narrow escape

「彼女は洪水から間一髪で逃れた」

解説 escapeの用法を問う問題。Aのescapeは「(危険など) を免れる」，Bのan escape routは「避難経路」，Cのmake one's escapeは「逃亡する」の意味。Dは「を間一髪で逃れる」の意味なので，had narrow escapeではなくhad a narrow escapeが正しい。Dが正解。

訳例 A. 幸運にも彼の家は火事を免れました。
B. 私はホテルでは必ず避難経路を確認することにしている。
C. 囚人は逃亡した。

80. 解答：C

with honor → with honors

「彼女は大学を優秀な成績で卒業した」

解説 honorの用法を問う問題。Aのdo the honorsは「名誉となる役割を務める」，Bのhave the honor ofは「(する) 光栄にあずかる」，Dのhonorは「を尊敬する，敬う」の意味。Cはgraduate with honorsで「優等で卒業する」の意味なので，with honorではなくwith honorsが正しい。Cが正解。

訳例 A. 結婚披露宴でスピーチをお願いできますか。
B. 彼は最優秀作家賞に選ばれる栄誉を得た。
D. 彼は自分を支えてくれた先生を尊敬している。

IX 300語前後のまとまりのある文を読み，読解力を試す問題。
空所補充，語句の並べ替え，語彙力，行間を読む力を問う問題を10問出題。

81. 解答：A

解説 "It joins the Korean words for 'moon' and 'enjoy.'" から，A が正解。

訳例 「ダヌリ」という名前はどういう意味ですか。

A. 月を楽しむ　B. 一緒に月へ行こう

C. 月はダヌリを楽しむだろう　D. 遠回りの燃費

82. 解答：D

解説 "Kwon Hyun-joon, director general of space and nuclear energy at South Korea's Ministry of Science," から，D が正解。

訳例 クォン・ヒョンジュンとは誰ですか。

A. 韓国の大統領　B. ジャーナリスト　C. 宇宙飛行士　D. 局長

83. 解答：C

解説 "Danuri was launched from Florida, setting out on a roundabout but fuel-efficient path to the moon." から，C が正解。

訳例 月に関する韓国省庁の当面の目標は何ですか。

A. 月に宇宙の植民地を作る。

B. 衛星を2年持たせる。

C. 遠回りだが燃費のいい月への道を作る。

D. ダヌリが任務を終えて地球に戻ってくること。

84. 解答：D

解説 "Danuri's mission includes ... and testing space Internet technology." から，D が正解。

訳例 ダヌリの主な仕事の1つは何ですか。

A. ダヌリはすでに月にいる人たちを助ける。

B. ダヌリは日本からの宇宙船に参加する。

C. ダヌリが月に着陸する。

D. ダヌリは宇宙インターネット技術をテストする。

85. 解答：D

解説 "Danuri will join spacecraft from the U.S. and India already operating around the moon, and a China rover exploring the moon's far side." から，D が正解。

訳例　本文によると，他にどのような国が月を探査していますか。

A. フランスとドイツ　　B. 日本と台湾

C. インドとロシア　　D. 中国とインド

86.　解答：C

解説　"The spacecraft's scientific payload will aid scientists in South Korea and around the world in ... and photographing craters at the lunar poles, where the sun never shines." から，C が正解。

訳例　ダヌリが科学者の月に対する理解を促すものを 1 つ挙げてください。

A. 月に存在した過去の生命を探すこと

B. 月で海を見つけること

C. 月の両極にあるクレーターの写真を撮ること

D. 月に住むことを学ぶこと

87.　解答：B

解説　"at the lunar poles, where the sun never shines." から，B が正解。

訳例　月の両極について述べられている重要なことは何ですか。

A. 両極は月で最も暖かい部分である。

B. 月の両極に太陽が当たることはない。

C. 月の磁力は両極で最も弱い。

D. 両極に人が住んでいた。

88.　解答：B

解説　"The moon's interior no longer generates a magnetic field, but it once did," から，B が正解。

訳例　過去の月の磁場について，どのようなことがわかっていますか。

A. 現在は磁場が強いが，過去には弱かった。

B. 昔は磁場が強かったが，いまはなくなっている。

C. 月の場所によって磁場が違う。

D. 月の磁場について科学者はほとんど知らない。

89.　解答：A

解説　"The moon's early magnetic field appears to have been surprisingly strong, possibly as much as double the strength of Earth's current magnetic field." から，A が正解。

訳例　過去の月の磁場について，どのようなことがわかっていますか。

A. 月の磁場は現在の地球の磁場の 2 倍の強さだった。

B. 月には固まった溶岩流がない。

C. かつて地球は月の周りを回っていた。

D. 古代の人々は月に火山があるのを見た。

90. 解答：C

解説　記事全体の内容によると，ダヌリが月の軌道に乗りそのミッションの内容について書かれているので，C が正解。

訳例　この記事に最もふさわしいタイトルは何ですか。

A. ダヌリは月に降り立つ！　B. ダヌリが月から戻ってくる！

C. ダヌリが月を周回する！　D. ダヌリが月に衝突する！

訳例　韓国は 2022 年 8 月 5 日（木）に，月周回衛星を搭載したロケットを打ち上げた。元々は「韓国月周回衛星」と呼ばれていたこのミッションは，命名コンテストの優勝作となった「ダヌリ」と名付けられた。韓国語の「月」と「楽しむ」を組み合わせたものである。

「私たちは，月を宇宙開発のための前哨基地として利用することも考えています」と韓国科学省の宇宙・原子力局長であるクォン・ヒョンジュン氏は述べた。「月そのものを探査することを望んでいますが，月が火星やその先の深宇宙探査の拠点となる可能性も認識しています」とつけ加えた。

ダヌリはフロリダから打ち上げられ，遠回りではあるが燃費のいい月への道を歩み出した。2022 年 12 月に地表から約 100km の高度で月の軌道に入る予定である。主なミッションは 1 年間を予定している。

ダヌリは，すでに月の周囲で活動している米国とインドの宇宙船，そして月の裏側を探査している中国の探査機と合流することになる。韓国の科学省によると，ダヌリのミッションには，将来の着陸地点の探索と宇宙インターネット技術のテストが含まれている。

この探査機の科学観測機器は，月の磁場の研究，ウラン，水，ヘリウム 3 などの元素や分子の量の測定，太陽が当たらない月の両極のクレーターの撮影などで，韓国をはじめ世界中の科学者を支援する。

ダヌリの最も重要な科学機器の 1 つが「磁力計」である。月の内部には磁場が存在しないが，かつては磁場があり，その古い磁場はその時代に固まった溶岩流に保存されている。月の初期の磁場は驚くほど強く，現在の地球磁場の 2 倍の強さであった可能性がある。

X

まとまりのある会話文を読み，会話が行われている状況におけるイディオム，語彙力，コミュニケーションの力を試す問題。10問出題。

91. 解答：C

解説 “It’s more straightforward than ‘climate change,’” から，C が正解。

訳例 ヨーコはなぜ「気候変動」ではなく「地球温暖化」を好んで使うのですか。

A. 彼女は季節の移り変わりが好きではない。

B. 彼女は寒い気候より暖かい気候の方が好きだ。

C. 生態系の危機をより正確に定義することができる。

D. かわいく聞こえる。

92. 解答：D

解説 “Well sure, some problems are not our problems. We’re not having huge forest fires here in Japan like in France or California.” とタローが述べていることから，D が正解。

訳例 フランスの森林火災について，タローはどう考えているのですか。

A. 森林火災は危険だ。

B. 森林火災はヨーコの問題だ。

C. 森林火災は地球温暖化が原因ではない。

D. 森林火災は彼の問題ではない。

93. 解答：A

解説 “You mean floods and forest fires are caused by climate change? I can’t imagine it!” とタローが尋ねたことに対して，“That’s what makes global warming so dangerous. People do not see connections.” とヨーコが述べていることから，A が正解。

訳例 ヨーコが言う地球温暖化による問題とは，巨大な森林火災の他に何がありますか。

A. ひどい洪水　B. 地球規模の問題に無関心ではない人たち

C. 地球の気温が急に下がること　D. 服が足りない

94. 解答：B

解説 “You mean floods and forest fires are caused by climate change? I can’t imagine it!” とタローが述べていることから，B が正解。

訳例 ひどい洪水について，タローはどう考えていますか。

A. 彼は日本だけの問題だと思っている。
B. 彼は地球温暖化が原因とは考えられない。
C. 彼はどうでもいいと思っている。
D. 彼は地球温暖化と関係があると思っている。

95. 解答：A

解説 "Do you know outdated women's fashion clothes are thrown on huge heaps that rot and increase the Earth's temperature?" とタローが地球温暖化は，婦人服も問題になっていると言ったことに対してヨーコは，タローが婦人服の問題を指摘することを予期していたと述べている。A が正解。

訳例 ヨーコが (95) "I know that was coming!" と言ったのはどういう意味ですか。
A. 彼女はタローが婦人服を非難することを予期していた。
B. 彼女は捨てられた服がタローのせいだとわかっていた。
C. 彼女はタローが自分に会いに来るだろうと予想していた。
D. 彼女は古着がすぐに自分に届けられることを知っていた。

96. 解答：B

解説 "For your information, many women are fighting against male-run clothing companies that are careless with the Earth's ecology." とヨーコが述べていることから，B が正解。

訳例 男性が経営するアパレル企業に関する女性の態度についてヨーコは何と言っていますか。
A. 女性たちはより多くの利益を上げるために企業を支援している。
B. 女性たちは，地球の生態系を傷つける無頓着な衣料品会社と闘っている。
C. 女性は，昇進できるから会社に満足している。
D. 女性たちは，自分たちとは関係ないから企業の方針に興味がない。

97. 解答：C

解説 "Women are redesigning old clothes or giving them to poor people." とヨーコが述べていることから，C が正解。

訳例 女性たちは時代遅れの婦人服をどうしているのでしょうか。
A. 女性たちはそれらを売って利益を上げている。
B. 女性たちはそれらを燃やして処分しています。
C. 女性たちはそれらをデザインし直したり，必要とする人々に与えたりしている。

D. 女性たちはそれらを積み上げて腐らせている。

98. 解答：D

解説 “The major problems are connected to overproduction and waste.” とヨーコが述べていることから，D が正解。

訳例 気候変動に関わる大きな問題について，ヨーコは何と言っていますか。

A. 気候変動に関心を持つ人が多すぎる。

B. 売ったり買ったりするものが少ない。

C. 気候変動と人々の過少消費を結びつけている。

D. 過剰生産と廃棄。

99. 解答：D

解説 “Because of that, the Earth is getting increasingly hotter and ecological systems are suffering.” とヨーコが述べていることから，D が正解。

訳例 地球温暖化の影響について，ヨーコは何と言っていますか。

A. 古くなった服を処分する女性が増えている。

B. 人々はお金のない生活を恐れている。

C. 地球温暖化が生態系に影響を与えると考える人は少なくなった。

D. 地球はますます高温になり，生態系は苦しんでいる。

100. 解答：A

解説 “The late Stephan Hawking was worried that the Earth would become so hot that people would need to search for other habitable planets.” から，A が正解。

訳例 故スティーヴン・ホーキング博士の懸念していたことは何でしたか。

A. 地球があまりに高温になり，人類は居住可能な他の惑星を探す必要がある。

B. 地球が他の惑星の人々によって占拠されてしまう。

C. 人々が地球の生態系を心配しすぎる。

D. 地球が熱くなりすぎて，人々はお金を稼ぐことに興味を失いそう。

訳例 タロー：今年の夏は日本が猛暑だね。これは気候変動の影響なのかな。

ヨーコ：私は「地球温暖化」がいいと思うわ。「気候変動」というより，もっと率直な表現だと思うの。気温の上昇は，それほど危険でもないし，自分たちの問題でもないと人に思わせてしまうかもしれないから。

タロー：まあ確かに，自分たちの問題ではないものもあるね。フランスやカリフォルニアのように，日本では大規模な山火事が起きているわけでもないしね。

ヨーコ：他の人の問題が自分たちの問題ということに気づかないことが間違っているわ。私たちはひどい洪水に見舞われているけど，それは気候変動，つまり地球温暖化が原因なのよ。

タロー：洪水や山火事が気候変動によって引き起こされるってこと？そんなこと想像もつかないよ。

ヨーコ：それが，地球温暖化の危険なところよ。人々は関連性に気づかないの。

タロー：時代遅れの女性ファッションの服が，巨大な山になって捨てられ腐敗して地球の温度を上昇させているのを知っているかい。

ヨーコ：そう来ると思っていたわ。ちなみに，男性が経営する地球のエコロジーに無頓着な衣料品会社に対抗して，多くの女性たちが闘っているのよ。女性たちは，古着をデザインし直したり，貧しい人たちにあげたりしているの。でも，あなたが今いま挙げたことは，最悪の気候問題の１つではないわ。主な問題は，過剰生産と廃棄に関連しているわ。そのせいで，地球はますます暑くなり，生態系は苦しんでいるのよ。

タロー：未来はどうなるんだろう。生態系が崩壊しそうで怖いなあ。

ヨーコ：あなただけじゃないわ。故スティーヴン・ホーキング博士は，地球があまりに高温になるため，他の居住可能な惑星を探さなければならなくなることを懸念していたの。

タロー：私たちが知っている惑星で，居住可能な惑星は他にないね。

ヨーコ：だから，地球の生態系を守ることが，私たちのいちばん大事な仕事なのよ。

2022年C級第2回試験　正解一覧

Ⅰ

1. C　2. A　3. D　4. B　5. A　6. C　7. B　8. C　9. D　10. A

Ⅱ

11. B　12. D　13. A　14. C　15. A　16. B　17. C　18. A　19. D　20. C

Ⅲ

21. B　22. C　23. B　24. B　25. D　26. C　27. C　28. A　29. D　30. B

Ⅳ

31. A　32. B　33. D　34. A　35. B　36. A　37. B　38. C　39. A　40. B

Ⅴ

41. C　42. A　43. D　44. B　45. B　46. B　47. C　48. A　49. D　50. D

Ⅵ

51. D　52. C　53. B　54. A　55. B　56. C　57. D　58. A　59. C　60. D

Ⅶ

61. C　62. D　63. A　64. A　65. B　66. B　67. D　68. D　69. B　70. C

Ⅷ

71. A　72. D　73. B　74. C　75. B　76. A　77. C　78. D　79. D　80. C

Ⅸ

81. A　82. D　83. C　84. D　85. D　86. C　87. B　88. B　89. A　90. C

Ⅹ

91. C　92. D　93. A　94. B　95. A　96. B　97. C　98. D　99. D　100. A

国連英検実施要項

（2023 年度時点）

主　　催	公益財団法人 日本国際連合協会 国連英検事務局
問い合わせ先	〒 104-0031　東京都中央区京橋 3-12-4 MAOビル 4 階 TEL 03-6228-6831 ／ FAX 03-6228-6832 http://www.kokureneiken.jp/

※国連英検 D 級・E 級は 2023 年度より開催を休止中。最新の実施情報は国連英検ホームページ http://www.kokureneiken.jp/ で必ず確認すること。

試験日

	1 次試験	2 次試験
第 1 回	毎年 5 月下旬の日曜日	毎年 7 月中旬の日曜日
第 2 回	毎年 10 月下旬の日曜日	毎年 12 月中旬の日曜日

※ 2 次試験は特 A 級・A 級のみ。

試験地

■ 1 次試験…札幌・仙台・さいたま・千葉・東京・神奈川・名古屋・神戸・京都・大阪・広島・福岡・鹿児島・那覇の予定

■ 2 次試験…特 A 級：東京・大阪

※特 A 級・A 級の併願者の 2 次試験はすべて東京・大阪で行なわれる。

A 級：札幌・仙台・東京・名古屋・大阪・福岡・那覇の予定

受験会場名，所在地は受験票に明示される。受験地の変更はできない。なお，1 次試験を特別会場で受験した受験者の 2 次試験は，最寄りの試験会場となる。

※開催最小人数に満たない会場は開催を中止する場合がある（1 次・2 次共）。

検定料（税込）

特 A 級…13,200 円　A 級…11,000 円

B 級…8,800 円　C 級…5,500 円

※一度納入された検定料は返却できない。申し込み後の変更もできない。

※事務局が申込書を検定料の受領後，受付完了。

併願受験検定料（税込）

特 A 級＋A 級＝ 22,000 円　A 級＋B 級＝ 17,600 円

B 級＋C 級＝ 13,200 円

※一度納入された検定料は返却できない。申し込み後の変更もできない。

※事務局が申込書を検定料の受領後，受付完了。

1 次試験の開始時間

A 級　C 級……午前 10 時 30 分（集合時間午前 10 時）

特 A 級　B 級……午後 2 時（集合時間午後 1 時 30 分）

試験内容

■ 1 次試験

級	試験方法	試験時間
特A・A	リーディング・英作文	120 分
B	リスニング・リーディング・英作文	120 分
C	リスニング・リーディング	100 分

■ 2 次試験

※特 A 級・A 級の 1 次試験合格者および 1 次試験免除者が対象。

※面接シートに事前に所要事項を英語で書き込み，外国人面接官などの質問事項に答える。

※ A 級については会場により Skype 等によるオンライン面接になる場合もある。

※面接の内容は試験実施の品質向上と厳正さを担保することを目的に録音（オンラインの場合は録画）される。

合格発表

合格者には合格カードを発行

試験結果は郵送にて通知。

	1 次試験	2 次試験
第 1 回	毎年 6 月下旬	毎年 8 月中旬
第 2 回	毎年 11 月下旬	毎年 1 月中旬

受験申し込み要項

●併願の場合

午前午後で隣接する 2 つの級を同日に受験することができる。併願を希望する場合は「受験申込書」の併願欄に記入して申し込むこと。

● 1 次試験免除

前回または前々回の 1 次試験に合格し，2 次試験に不合格または欠席した場合，申請により 1 次試験が免除され，2 次試験のみ受験できる。申込書の所定欄にその旨を記入し申し込むこと。検定料は同じ。

受験票

申込書と検定料金の受理後，受験地の会場・所在地が記載された受験票が 1 次試験日の 1 週間前までに送付される。届かない場合は，必ず試験日の 3 日前までに国連英検事務局（03-6228-6831〈代表〉）へ問い合わせること。顔写真 1 枚（4 センチ× 3 センチ）を試験日までに用意し受験票に貼り付けておくこと。試験当日は，受験票とともに身分証明書を持参すること。

受験申し込み方法

書店，郵送，インターネット（PC・スマートフォン）で申し込みができる。
詳細は国連英検ホームページ http://www.kokureneiken.jp/ で確認する。

申込受付期間

第 1 回　3 月初旬～ 4 月下旬　※翌日消印有効
第 2 回　8 月初旬～ 9 月下旬　※翌日消印有効

検定料のお支払い方法

電話で申し込む場合	国連英検事務局へ電話・FAX にて申し込みができる。申し込み受付後「コンビニ支払用紙」が郵送される。
郵送で申し込む場合	国連英検事務局に受験申込書を請求する。 ●支払方法：必ず受験者氏名で銀行または郵便局から振り込む。
インターネット（PC・スマートフォン）で申し込む場合	国連英検のホームページから申し込みができる。 （PC・スマートフォン）http://www.kokureneiken.jp/ ●支払方法：クレジットカード支払い，コンビニエンスストア支払い，銀行または郵便局から振り込む。

検定料の各種支払詳細

振込の場合	**●銀行からの振込** 銀行名：　三菱 UFJ 銀行　日本橋支店 口座名：　（公財）日本国際連合協会　国連英検事務局 口座番号：普通口座 0010400 金額：　　該当級の受験料 ※振込手数料は受験者負担。 ※現金・為替は取り扱い不可。 ※いずれも事務局が申込書と検定料の受領を確認後，受付完了。 ※インターネット（PC・スマートフォン）で申し込んだ受験者は，ご依頼人の前に「受付番号」（メールにて通知される）を記入する。
	●郵便局からの払込 郵便局設置の払込書（青票）にて以下の内容を記入の上，払い込む。 加入者名：（公財）日本国際連合協会 口座番号：00130-7-24670 金額：　　該当級の受験料 ※振込手数料は受験者負担。 ※ご依頼人欄に受験者名，住所，電話番号を必ず記入する。インターネット（PC・スマートフォン）で申し込んだ受験者は，ご依頼人の前に「受付番号」（メールにて通知される）を記入する。 ※払込金受領書は必ず保管する。
クレジットカードの場合	**●インターネット（PC・スマートフォン）からの申し込みのみ可能** 入力フォームにて「クレジットカード払い」を選択し，カード番号，有効期限などを入力する。 ※利用可能クレジットカードは国連英検のホームページで確認のこと。
コンビニエンスストアの場合	●インターネット（PC・スマートフォン）からの申し込みの場合 入力フォームにて「コンビニ払い」を選択すると，払込票が送付される。 ●電話・FAX で申し込みの場合 申し込み受付完了後事務局より「コンビニ支払用紙」が郵送される。 ※全国の主要なコンビニエンスストアにて受験料を支払う。

著者・執筆協力者プロフィール

著　者

谷 山 澤 子（たにやま・さわこ）
元神戸女子短期大学教授。文学博士。国連英検指導検討委員会委員。著書に『国連英検 B 級・C 級対策［改訂版］』（共著，三修社）など多数。

Alexander Shishin（アレキサンダー・シシン）
神戸女子大学名誉教授。文学博士。国連英検指導検討委員会委員。著書に『国連英検 B 級・C 級対策［改訂版］』（共著，三修社）など多数。

執筆協力者

服 部 孝 彦（はっとり・たかひこ）
大妻女子大学・同大学院教授。言語学博士。国連英検統括監修官。著書に『国連英検ベーシック・トライアル』（三修社）など多数。

リスニング問題の音声ダウンロードのご案内

リスニング問題の音声については、PC、スマートフォン等で以下の国連英検ウェブサイトから再生またはダウンロードして下さい。

【音声提供 URL】

http://www.kokureneiken.jp/dist/listening/

CD をご希望の場合

PC やスマートフォンでの音声データの取り扱いについてよく分からないという方は CD-R をお送りしますので国連英検事務局までお問い合わせ下さい。

【連絡先】

公益財団法人 日本国際連合協会 国連英検事務局 宛

TEL 03-6228-6831　FAX 03-6228-6832　URL http://www.kokureneiken.jp/

国連英検過去問題集《こくれんえいけんかこもんだいしゅう》［C級《しーきゅう》］〈2021-2022年度実施《ねんどじっし》〉

2023年7月31日　第1刷発行

編　者　公益財団法人　日本国際連合協会
著　者　谷山澤子　アレキサンダー・シシン
執筆協力　服部孝彦
発行者　前田俊秀
発行所　株式会社三修社
〒150-0001 東京都渋谷区神宮前2-2-22
TEL 03-3405-4511 FAX 03-3405-4522
振替 00190-9-72758
https://www.sanshusha.co.jp
印刷・製本　日経印刷株式会社
編集協力／大嶋晶代
装丁デザイン／仁井谷伴子

ISBN978-4-384-06076-8 C2082